NEW DIRECTIONS FOR PROGRAM EVALUATION
A Publication of the American Evaluation Association

William R. Shadish, *Memphis State University*
EDITOR-IN-CHIEF

Program Evaluation: A Pluralistic Enterprise

Lee Sechrest
University of Arizona

EDITOR

Number 60, Winter 1993

JOSSEY-BASS PUBLISHERS
San Francisco

PROGRAM EVALUATION: A PLURALISTIC ENTERPRISE
Lee Sechrest (ed.)
New Directions for Program Evaluation, no. 60
William R. Shadish, Editor-in-Chief

Microfilm copies of issues and articles are available in 16mm and 35mm,
as well as microfiche in 105mm, through University Microfilms Inc., 300
North Zeeb Road, Ann Arbor, Michigan 48106-1346.

LC 85-644749   ISSN 0164-7989   ISBN 1-55542-679-4

NEW DIRECTIONS FOR PROGRAM EVALUATION is part of The Jossey-Bass
Education Series and is published quarterly by Jossey-Bass Inc., Publishers
(publication number USPS 449-050).

EDITORIAL CORRESPONDENCE should be sent to the editor-in-chief,
William R. Shadish, Department of Psychology, Memphis State University,
Memphis, Tennessee 38152.

Manufactured in the United States of America. Nearly all Jossey-Bass
books, jackets, and periodicals are printed on recycled paper that contains
at least 50 percent recycled waste, including 10 percent postconsumer
waste. Many of our materials are also printed with vegetable-based ink;
during the printing process these inks emit fewer volatile organic com-
pounds (VOCs) than petroleum-based inks. VOCs contribute to the formation of smog.

Instructions to Contributors

NEW DIRECTIONS FOR PROGRAM EVALUATION (NDPE), a quarterly sourcebook, is an official publication of the American Evaluation Association. As such, NDPE publishes empirical, methodological, and theoretical work on all aspects of program evaluation and related fields. Substantive areas may include any area of social programming such as mental health, education, job training, medicine, or public health, but may also extend the boundaries of evaluation to such topics as product evaluation, personnel evaluation, policy analysis, or technology assessment. In all cases, the focus on evaluation is more important than the particular substantive topic.

NDPE does not consider or publish unsolicited single manuscripts. Each issue of NDPE is devoted to a single topic, with contributions solicited, organized, reviewed, and edited by a guest editor. Issues may take any of several forms, such as a series of related chapters, a monograph, or a long article followed by brief critical commentaries. In all cases, proposals must follow a specific format, which can be obtained from the editor-in-chief. These proposals are sent to members of the editorial board, and to relevant substantive experts, for peer review. This process may result in rejection, acceptance, or a recommendation to revise and resubmit. However, NDPE is committed to working constructively with potential guest editors to help them develop acceptable proposals. Close contact with the editor-in-chief is encouraged during proposal preparation and generation.

COPIES OF NDPE's "Guide for Proposal Development" and "Proposal Format" can be obtained from the editor-in-chief:

William R. Shadish, Editor-in-Chief
New Directions for Program Evaluation
Department of Psychology
Memphis State University
Memphis, TN 38152
Office: 901-678-4687
FAX: 901-678-2579
Bitnet: SHADISHWR@MEMSTVX1

CONTENTS

Editor's Notes

The contents of this volume represent unusually important and lucid contributions to our understanding of the extent to which research, including program evaluation, must be considered a plural enterprise. Together, the chapters by Shadish and Cordray also show how advantage increases if pluralism is planned and deliberate, whether at the stage of formulating problems and conducting research or at the stage of synthesizing and interpreting the findings of multiple studies. No single study is likely to yield findings that we should consider definitive. The same can probably be said of program evaluations. Certainly no single study can teach us much of what we need to know. The introductory remarks by Figueredo in Chapter One neatly tie together the overall strategies of critical multiplism and meta-analysis and relate them both to generalizability theory. This volume is aimed at helping us to plan our research in a way that maximizes the return on the time and effort that we have invested in it.

Chapters Two and Three in this volume were originally prepared for conferences, and they were published in conference proceedings that had very limited distribution and virtually none in the program evaluation field. Both authors have substantially revised and updated their original papers to maximize their current value. Readers will, I think, enjoy them as intellectual products and benefit greatly from giving their methodological recommendations a careful hearing.

Lee Sechrest
Editor

LEE SECHREST is professor of psychology at the University of Arizona.

This chapter examines the conceptual relationships between the research strategy of critical multiplism and the methods of meta-analysis and generalizability theory for quantitative data synthesis.

Critical Multiplism, Meta-analysis, and Generalization: An Integrative Commentary

Aurelio José Figueredo

In Chapter Two of this volume, Shadish describes and defends the research strategy of critical multiplism. Critical multiplism can be characterized as the strategy that systematically extends and applies the principles of multiple operationalism (Campbell and Fiske, 1959) to all components of the research enterprise. Just as we deem that any single measure of a hypothetical construct is fallible and subject to systematic method bias, we must also acknowledge that any single research method or procedure (collectively called *research tactics*) is equally limited. Thus, multiple operationalism can be viewed as the application of critical multiplism to the problem of fallible measurement. Shadish identifies several components of the research process to which multiplism can and should be applied: question formation, theory or model selection, research design, data analysis, and interpretation of results.

The application of critical multiplism to certain components of the research process can be identified with certain familiar methodological doctrines. For example, in question formation, critical multiplism can be seen as addressing both the threat of confirmation bias (Greenwald, Pratkanis, Leippe, and Baumgardner, 1983) and certain aspects of the problem of incommensurability (Feyerabend, 1975). In theory or model selection, critical multiplism can be equated with the method of multiple working hypotheses (Chamberlin, 1890) or strong inference (Platt, 1964). In research design, critical multiplism can be seen as the premeditated equivalent of the progressive effect of competing scientific research programs

(Lakatos, 1970, 1978) or rival research traditions (Laudan, 1977). Such historical continuities make critical multiplism more, rather than less, useful as a broad integrative framework for contemporary methodology. The fact that the proposed unified system contains many familiar elements should increase confidence, not invite dismissal.

Shadish notes that critical multiplism can be implemented at one or both of two levels: the individual level and the institutional level. At the individual level, the individual researcher must take the trouble to implement critical multiplist strategies in any given study, so that the validity of his or her inferences from the study will be strengthened. At the institutional level, the population of researchers constituting any given portion of the scientific community must foster multiplicity in their research tactics, so that valid inferences can be drawn from the scientific literature as a whole if not necessarily from individual studies. At the institutional level, both the individual study and the individual researcher are considered fallible and biased instruments of which nothing more can be expected. Shadish reviews the various social psychological, motivational, and economic constraints on the practice of critical multiplism at the individual level and concludes that, for the present, it can be recommended only tentatively at that level. Although he acknowledges that institutional barriers can also exist, he nevertheless strongly endorses the immediate implementation of critical multiplism at the institutional level. Unproductive pseudoproblems and polemics, such as the current dispute between qualitative and quantitative approaches in program evaluation, would thus be rendered moot (Sechrest, 1992).

Given the literature documenting the intellectual vices of confirmation bias and the consequences of paradigmatic tunnel vision in the history of science (Greenwald, Pratkanis, Leippe, and Baumgardner, 1983), a stronger case can and should be made for the implementation of critical multiplism at the individual level. While the pettiness and egomania of certain researchers may hamper this effort, there is no reason to believe that at least some of us are not capable of rising above these limitations and aspiring to this worthy ideal (Chamberlin, 1890). Critical multiplism warns us that we may be biased in various ways as individual researchers, but it also counsels us that such bias is no justification for either intentionally cultivating our limitations or tolerating those failings in others. A consistent meliorist position would be to do what we can both as individuals and as parts of a collective.

Nevertheless, it is clearly easier for the implementation of critical multiplism to start at the institutional level. There are two alternative ways of accomplishing this: proactively or retroactively. Shadish argues for a proactive position, as exemplified by the expression *planned critical multiplism* (Shadish, 1986). He contrasts this with a mindless multiplism that introduces methodological heterogeneities uncritically at the individual level for no apparent reason and with no particular purpose in mind. However, there is one way in which multiplism can be both critical and retroactive at the institutional level, and that is in the field of meta-analysis. In Chapter Three of this volume, Cordray, although not explicitly addressing the problems of critical multiplism, describes how modern techniques of meta-analysis can be used for these purposes.

Meta-analysis represents an emerging technology for the quantitative review of research literature. The purpose of meta-analysis is twofold: the data synthesis of homogeneous results and the causal analysis of discrepant results. Data synthesis of homogeneous results involves first testing for homogeneity of effect sizes, then pooling results across studies. The main functions of data synthesis are the estimation of population effect sizes and the enhancement of statistical power by the pooling of data to detect these effects. Data synthesis has one major problem: It often rejects statistical homogeneity, an indication of discrepant results. As with all null hypothesis testing, it is usually no more than a matter of achieving sufficient statistical power to obtain a statistically significant result. Thus, that the pooling of results in data synthesis has the twin objectives of estimating parameters of population effect sizes and testing for the significance of homogeneous effects across studies may be self-defeating.

When discrepant results are obtained, causal analysis looks carefully at the designs of the different studies. These design features represent the "local molar conditions" (Campbell, 1986, p. 69) under which the discrepant results were obtained. Causal analysis is accomplished by structural modeling of the reported effects. The function of causal analysis is to determine whether results can be generalized across study conditions by capitalizing on the "heterogeneity of irrelevancies" (Cook, 1993, p. 50) between individual studies. Thus, meta-analysis can be used retroactively to implement critical multiplism at the institutional level by the quantitative analysis of research results (General Accounting Office, 1992). As Cordray points out in Chapter Three, this meta-analytic enterprise is observational in nature, whether or not the individual studies sampled are experimental. Thus, meta-analysis can be thought of as an exercise in retroactive, a posteriori, critical multiplism at the institutional level.

Cordray reviews the various vulnerabilities to which meta-analysis is subject as a nonexperimental procedure by recapitulating some of the threats to primary analysis of nonexperimental data and applying the same logic to the planning of meta-analysis. These threats to validity include variable errors, such as sampling errors, processing errors, and coding errors; systematic errors relating to sampling issues, such as small-sample bias and frame bias; systematic errors relating to nonsampling issues, such as noncoverage of subgroups and the influence of inclusion rules on generalization; and nonresponse and missing data, such as field errors and processing errors of this type. He finds that each type of error experienced in primary nonexperimental research can be duplicated at the meta-analytic level and that each has been acknowledged as a potential threat in the meta-analytic literature. However, Cordray is repeatedly drawn to the errors that often underlie the primary analyses on which the meta-analysis is ultimately based and that it may merely be reflecting. Thus, although meta-analysts can, of course, make errors of their own, it is possible that many of the major threats to meta-analysis consist either of repeating or of not compensating for the known limitations of the primary research.

Thus, the validity of meta-analytic results is contingent on the implementation of critical multiplist strategies at the institutional level, the alternative being a meta-analytic strategy of mindless multiplism that aggregates data without regard to the conditions under which they were obtained. Furthermore, this corrective action is often necessitated by the inadequate implementation of a priori critical multiplist strategies at the level of individual researchers. Any task or component of the research process left homogeneous at the meta-analytic level constitutes a potential threat to the validity of the meta-analysis. This fact implies that critical multiplist strategies of data synthesis at the institutional level are a requirement.

There is one other way in which meta-analysis can go beyond mere synthesis of the published results of primary data analyses. Typically, meta-analytic models are directed to the systematic variations in a single effect across multiple studies. Thus, although there may be multiple meta-analytic predictors, the criterial effect size remains essentially univariate. However, instead of limiting the scope of the meta-analysis to a single effect, we can extend meta-analytic techniques to reconstruct the broad pattern of relationships among the relevant variables. Thus, we can synthesize a correlation matrix from a sample of studies reporting either different sets or individual estimates of bivariate correlations. Each correlational element in the synthesized matrix represents an estimate of population effect size obtained by pooling across multiple studies, but no single study needs to report data on all the requisite relationships. We can then construct a structural equations model for this system of relationships at the population level that would not have been possible if we had used only the data from an individual study. Thus, the whole body of literature can yield more than the simple sum (or even the weighted average) of its parts, qualitatively as well as quantitatively, while the individual study can constitute a single piece of a larger mosaic (Schmidt, 1992).

For example, many studies of treatment compliance report the various predictors of compliance, whereas others report only the various effects of compliance on treatment outcomes. The problem with this piecemeal approach is that many predictors of poor compliance are also likely to predict poor treatment outcomes. Thus, from the results of any single study, we usually cannot discriminate the direct effects of such predictors on outcomes from the indirect effects mediated through poor compliance. In fact, some studies (Coronary Drug Project Research Group, 1980; Yeaton, 1990) have shown that the significant predictors of compliance are systematically associated with poor treatment outcomes even in the control (that is, placebo) condition, where compliance simply cannot be materially causal. By meta-analytically synthesizing the full correlation matrix needed, we might be able to construct the requisite path model to estimate and test separately both the direct and the indirect effects of such predictors on treatment outcomes. Thus, the complex role of such important constructs in evaluation research as treatment compliance can be understood in the context of other relevant causal influences. This type of application represents yet another way in which meta-analysis can be used to implement critical multiplist strategies retroactively at the institutional level.

However, both Cordray and Shadish go beyond the uses of meta-analysis as a merely retroactive implementation of critical multiplism. They both propose that, by assessing the limitations of the scientific literature as a whole, we can plan future research strategically to compensate for specific gaps that we have identified in the collective empirical findings of a field. Thus, an individual study can be designed to foster critical multiplism at the population level by preferentially utilizing alternatives to the mainstream procedures. Rather than deviating capriciously for the sake of mere novelty, the individual researcher can strategically plan a study a posteriori to compensate for gaps in collective knowledge that quantitative data synthesis has revealed. Thus, individual researchers can practice a kind of affirmative action for underutilized tactical elements that promise to answer important empirical questions in the field. The scientific value of an individual study is therefore better assessed in relation to what it adds to the cumulative literature than in relation to what it might add by itself. Although these guiding principles may appear to be intuitively obvious, they do not now dominate attitudes toward research design in the social and behavioral sciences. Currently, any substantial deviation in research tactics has to be explicitly justified in peer review, however plausible it may be.

Taken together, Chapters Two and Three go a long way toward identifying major challenges and charting a promising new course for both qualitative and quantitative research methodology in the coming years. However, there are ways in which we can go beyond them to explore future directions for this general line of inquiry. For example, the literature has failed to address some additional threats to the external validity of meta-analytic models. These threats include violations of independence between replications, as when a meta-analytic sample contains multiple studies by a single researcher, by multiple researchers from a single "laboratory," and by multiple "laboratories" within a single research paradigm. Another, related threat that the literature has not sufficiently explored is the consequences of correlated design features across studies. This condition produces multicollinearity of meta-analytic predictors, and it therefore introduces uncertainty or ambiguity of causal inference—a threat to the internal validity of the meta-analytic structural model. Moreover, because the retroactive critical multiplism of meta-analysis depends on the naturally occurring heterogeneity of irrelevancies in the research literature, failure to examine systematic homogeneities in the primary data critically constitutes a major threat to the entire meta-analytic enterprise in relation to the generalizability of causal inference.

Figueredo and Scott (1992) have proposed that, in addition to conventional meta-analysis, which they distinguish as effects meta-analysis, we develop a parallel technology for contents meta-analysis. Effects meta-analysis would continue to serve the function of causal analysis of discrepant results by creating structural models for variable effects, but it would otherwise remain subject to the limitations of the dominant research paradigms. In contrast, contents meta-analysis would be analogous to the content analysis of text, focusing as it would purely on the selection of methods, not on the results of individual studies. Appropriate techniques would include either exploratory or confirmatory factor analysis of correlated design features developing measurement models for what could be described as research paradigm constructs. Although many authors (Feyerabend, 1975; Laudan, 1977; Lakatos, 1970, 1978) have tried to define precisely what is meant by *research paradigm* since Kuhn (1970) first formulated the notion, the idea that individual scientific tactics (as Shadish understands the term in Chapter Two) are typically not independent but form discriminable constellations of related elements is common to most conceptions. An empirical approach to the study of these hypothetical metascientific constructs is to look for the stochastically predicted clusters of intercorrelated tactical elements meta-analytically in the methodological contents of published research. Although this multivariate operationalization of a research paradigm does not exhaust the concept, it does appear to be at least consistent with most of the variant formulations of the way in which research paradigms operate, and it should therefore be serviceable for the basic purposes of measurement.

Moreover, by combining the techniques of contents and effects meta-analysis, we could relate the methodological contents of studies to the magnitudes of the effects reported. Thus, the paradigm constructs would serve as latent predictors for structural models, providing both data reduction for the meta-analytic model predictors (which often exceed our usable sample size) and the statistical control of any spurious multicollinearity between them. We would accomplish this task by developing what we could call *meta-analytic factor analytic structural equation models* (Scott, Figueredo, and Hendrix, 1992; Bentler, 1989). Thus, by using these two meta-analytic techniques in combination, we could determine empirically not only whether research paradigms existed as theoretically specified but what their parameters were as defined by their constituent tactical elements and the biasing impact that their systematic perturbations of effect size could have on our collective results. By providing a firmer evidential foundation for the concept of a research paradigm, this empirical approach might also help to prevent or at least limit the increasing trivialization of a useful metascientific concept by profligate and inflated uses that refer it to relatively minor variations in research tactics, vaguely defined ideological "movements," or transient methodological fads.

Another future direction that I think is promising is in the complementary applications of generalizability theory and meta-analysis in program evaluation (Figueredo, Scott, and McKnight, 1993). Although generalizability theory (Cronbach, Gleser, Nanda, and Rajaratnam, 1972) and meta-analytic studies (Hedges and Olkin, 1985) can both be represented mathematically as variance component models within the general framework of hierarchical linear models (Bryk and Raudenbush, 1992), differences in emphasis produce a gap. Current meta-analytic models emphasize the structural explanation of the systematic divergences between studies where heterogeneities exist, whereas data synthesis can only pool statistically homogeneous results. Because they consider different studies to be multiple levels of an additional facet, generalizability models, which also provide information about these differences, enable us to quantify the degree of relative convergence over the sampled levels of any facet and thus even between partially discrepant studies. For that reason, we might even be able to pool moderately heterogeneous results, with caution, if we use associated generalizability coefficients computed across the specified structural dimensions of difference to qualify our results. Just as we routinely report sample means and qualify them by associated standard deviations, we might be able to report more global estimates of effect size and qualify them by estimates of the systematic variability that can be expected across studies. Thus, the basic difference between these two approaches can be seen as an emphasis on parameter estimation rather than hypothesis testing in the structural models. Therefore, by the complementary application of generalizability theory, meta-analysis can avoid the intellectual cul-de-sac into which institutionalized Fisherian null hypothesis testing the social sciences has often led it (Meehl, 1978).

One other interesting contrast that might produce added complications in model specification, estimation, and testing dovetails with the concerns of contents meta-analysis. Currently, most generalizability models are developed for the results of single-researcher or single-research-group experiments. If we consider researchers as another possible facet for generalizability analysis, as the logic of critical multiplism implies that we should, the researcher facet is typically either fully crossed with all other facets or constant across them. In a meta-analytic application of generalizability analysis, the researcher facet would be at least partially confounded with other facets of research design, because individual researchers may idiosyncratically study different aspects of the same general problem. Even if individual researchers are represented by multiple studies in the meta-analytic sample, multiple studies conducted by the same researchers are likely to share many design features due either to individual expertise or to theoretical orientation.

Thus, a hierarchical analytical strategy analogous to a split-plot design might be appropriate. Under such a strategy, systematic interindividual differences would be statistically controlled by a subjects factor for individual researchers. The variable design features of multiple studies by individual researchers could be represented by one or more within-subjects factors, and any larger classes or groupings of researchers, such as those associated with theoretical orientations or research paradigms, could be represented by one or more between-subjects factors. The resulting problems in model specification, estimation, and testing would be the high correlations that we might expect between the researcher factors and the study characteristics factors. The finding of Shadish and Sweeney (1991) that behavioral therapists disproportionately tend to use behavioral measures of outcome provides a good example. Another possible solution is to include only one study per individual researcher in the meta-analytic sample and not even attempt to discriminate between researchers and associated design features. However, this would merely mask the confound and not solve the problem. This problem is related to the problem posed by research paradigms that can be addressed by contents (as opposed to effects) meta-analysis. Contents meta-analysis studies the constellations of correlated design features independently of the outcome effects.

In conclusion, meta-analysis can ideally serve as a retroactive or a posteriori application of critical multiplism at the institutional level, pending a more widespread application of critical multiplism at the individual level. However, to accomplish this ambitious task, meta-analysis must eventually address the related problems of nonindependence of individual studies and correlated design features produced by the purported existence of internally homogeneous research paradigms. Complementary techniques that would explicitly include such broad metascientific concerns within the scope of meta-analysis have been proposed in this chapter. Such tactical extensions could function in the way in which certain correlational techniques were joined with existing experimental techniques to create the field of quasi-experimentation (Cook and Campbell, 1979; Cordray, 1986). Instead of merely criticizing the potential limitations of meta-analysis, as we used to criticize confounded or "flawed" experiments before quantitative quasi-experimental techniques were developed, we could then control directly for specifiable threats.

References

Bentler, P. M. EQS: Structural Equations Program Manual. Los Angeles: BMDP Statistical Software, 1989.

Bryk, A. S., and Raudenbush, S. W. Hierarchical Linear Models: Applications and Data Analysis Methods. Newbury Park, Calif.: Sage, 1992.

Campbell, D. T. "Relabeling Internal and External Validity for Applied Social Scientists." In W.M.K. Trochim (ed.), Advances in Quasi-Experimental Design and Analysis. New Directions for Program Evaluation, no. 31. San Francisco: Jossey-Bass, 1986.

Campbell, D. T., and Fiske, D. W. "Convergent and Discriminant Validation by the Multitrait-Multimethod Matrix." Psychological Bulletin, 1959, 56, 81–105.

Chamberlin, T. C. "The Method of Multiple Working Hypotheses." Science, 1890, 15, 92.

Cook, T. D. "A Quasi-Sampling Theory of the Generalization of Causal Relations." In L. B. Sechrest and A. G. Scott (eds.), Understanding Causes and Generalizing About Them. New Directions for Program Evaluation, no. 57. San Francisco: Jossey-Bass, 1993.

Cook, T. D., and Campbell, D. T. Quasi-experimentation: Design and Analysis Issues for Field Settings. Boston: Houghton Mifflin, 1979.

Cordray, D. S. "Quasi-experimental Analysis: A Mixture of Methods and Judgement." In W.M.K. Trochim (ed.), Advances in Quasi-experimental Design and Analysis. New Directions for Program Evaluation, no. 31. San Francisco: Jossey-Bass, 1986.

Coronary Drug Project Research Group. "Influence of Adherence to Treatment and Response of Cholesterol on Mortality in the Coronary Drug Project." New England Journal of Medicine, 1980, 303, 1038–1041.

Cronbach, L. J., Gleser, G., Nanda, H., and Rajaratnam, N. The Dependability of Behavioral Measurements: Theory of Generalizability for Scores and Profiles. New York: Wiley, 1972.

Feyerabend, P. Against Method: Outline of an Anarchistic Theory of Knowledge. London: Verso, 1975.

Figueredo, A. J., and Scott, A. G. "An Example of Contents Meta-analysis and Its Use in Higher Education Retention Studies." Paper presented at the American Evaluation Association Annual Meeting, Seattle, 1992.

Figueredo, A. J., Scott, A. G., and McKnight, P. E. "Complementary Applications of Generalizability Theory and Meta-analysis in Program Evaluation." Paper presented at the Canadian Evaluation Society Conference, Banff, Alberta, 1993.

General Accounting Office. Cross Design Synthesis: A New Strategy for Medical Effectiveness Research. GAO/PEMD 92–18. Washington, D.C.: GAO, 1992.

Greenwald, A. G., Pratkanis, A. R., Leippe, M. R., and Baumgardner, M. H. "Under What Conditions Does Theory Obstruct Research Progress?" Psychological Review, 1983, 93, 216–229.

Hedges, L. V., and Olkin, I. Statistical Methods for Meta-analysis. New York: Academic Press, 1985.

Kuhn, T. S. The Structure of Scientific Revolutions. (2nd ed.) Chicago: University of Chicago Press, 1970.

Lakatos, I. "Falsification and the Methodology of Scientific Research Programs." In I. Lakatos and A. Musgrave (eds.), Criticism and the Growth of Knowledge. Cambridge, England: Cambridge University Press, 1970.

Lakatos, I. The Methodology of Scientific Research Programs. Cambridge, England: Cambridge University Press, 1978.

Laudan, L. Progress and Its Problems: Towards a Theory of Scientific Growth. Berkeley: University of California Press, 1977.

Meehl, P. E. "Theoretical Risks and Tabular Asterisks: Sir Karl, Sir Ronald, and the Slow Progress of Soft Psychology." Journal of Consulting and Clinical Psychology, 1978, 46, 806–834.

Platt, J. R. "Strong Inference." *Science,* 1964, *146,* 347–353.

Schmidt, F. L. "What Do Data Really Mean? Research Findings, Meta-analysis, and Cumulative Knowledge in Psychology." *American Psychologist,* 1992, *47,* 1173–1181.

Scott, A. G., Figueredo, A. J., and Hendrix, J. "Meta-analysis of Research in Higher Education Retention Studies." Paper presented at the American Evaluation Association Annual Meeting, Seattle, 1992.

Sechrest, L. "Roots: Back to Our First Generations." *Evaluation Practice,* 1992, *13,* 1–7.

Shadish, W. R. "Planned Critical Multiplism: Some Elaborations." *Behavioral Assessment,* 1986, *8,* 75–103.

Shadish, W. R., and Sweeney, R. B. "Mediators and Moderators in Meta-analysis: There's a Reason We Don't Let Dodo Birds Tell Us Which Psychotherapies Should Have Prizes." *Journal of Consulting and Clinical Psychology,* 1991, *59,* 883–893.

Yeaton, W. H. "Causal Power: Strengthening Causal Claims Using No-Difference Findings." In L. Sechrest, E. Perrin, and J. Bunker (eds.), *Research Methodology: Strengthening Causal Interpretations of Nonexperimental Data.* Washington, D.C.: Agency for Health Care Policy and Research, U.S. Department of Health and Human Services, 1990.

AURELIO JOSÉ FIGUEREDO is associate professor of psychology at the University of Arizona.

Recent debates suggest that quantitative and qualitative approaches to evaluation are inevitably separated by a gap in worldviews. Critical multiplism is one way of thinking about evaluation that can unify these two approaches.

Critical Multiplism: A Research Strategy and Its Attendant Tactics

William R. Shadish

The quantitative-qualitative debate continues to split the house of evaluation. To their deepest adversaries, quantitative evaluators are all logical positivists ignorant of modern philosophy using outmoded methods. To their most steadfast opponents, qualitative evaluators are soft-headed radical constructivists who deny the concepts of reality and truth and so unwittingly deny the truth of their own approach. Despite the best efforts of those who have tried to unite the warring factions (Cook and Reichardt, 1979), such stereotyped interactions persist, and skirmishes between the interested parties regularly flare up into full-scale wars.

Central to the continued schism, I think, is the perception that quantitative and qualitative evaluators lack a common philosophical ground on which to meet. This chapter describes such a common ground, a unifying research strategy that all parties may be able to live with even if they do not endorse all its particulars. The strategy is not beyond criticism. In fact, criticism is one of its central tenets, so it welcomes criticism, and criticism is consistent with it. Nor will this strategy tell evaluators the right way to do things. In fact, it is premised on the notion that there rarely is one right way, so the best we can do is to try many ways while criticizing each. It is merely a way of moving us one step ahead of many current fruitless debates

This chapter is a substantial revision of a paper that appeared under the same title in L. Sechrest, H. Freeman, and A. Mulley (eds.), *Health Services Research Methodology: A Focus on AIDS*. DHHS Publication No. (PHS) 89–3439. Rockville, Md.: National Center for Health Services Research and Health Care Technology Assessment, Public Health Service, U.S. Department of Health and Human Services, 1989.

about paradigms. These debates are fruitless in no small part because of their continued obsession with a dead philosophy: logical positivism.

Logical Positivism Is Dead

It is fashionable to attack logical positivism these days, and it is easy to guess why: Logical positivism is dead, so one is sure to win. As Paul Meehl (1986, p. 315) pointed out, "logical positivism, in anything like the sense of Vienna in the late twenties, turned out not to be logically defensible, or even rigorously formulatable, by its adherents. It is epistemologically unsound from a variety of viewpoints (including ordinary language analysis); it is not an accurate picture of the structure of advanced sciences, such as physics; and it is grossly inadequate as a reconstruction of empirical history of science. So it is dead. All old surviving logical positivists agree, including my friend and teacher Feigl, who invented the phrase *logical positivism* and [who] was the first to introduce the approach in the United States in 1931. The last remaining defender of anything like logical positivism was Gustav Bergmann, who ceased to do so by the late 1940s." Such disavowals ought to alert us that something is seriously wrong with any argument that treats logical positivism as if it were still a credible philosophical opponent. Put this way, many evaluators would agree.

But another argument is often forwarded to justify the continued focus on the flaws of logical positivism, namely that many evaluators or evaluation clients are implicit logical positivists. As one respected colleague put it in a recent conversation, what else would you call someone who believes that evaluation methods can yield definitive answers about the true state of affairs in a program? Admittedly, such a person could be called an implicit logical positivist if he or she assumed, for instance, that our methods can yield definitive answers. The problem with this reasoning, however, is that such assumptions are implicitly consistent with a host of approaches to science, not just with logical positivism. On closer examination, it makes much more sense to think of these assumptions as coming from some influence other than logical positivism, for two reasons. First, these implicit logical positivists almost never display knowledge of other aspects of logical positivism that are much more closely tied to the position. For instance, I have yet to see such a person endorse the use of predicate logic as a means of adjudicating theoretical disputes, although that is the logic in logical positivism (Bechtel, 1988). If they were logical positivists at all, surely they would know this. Second, such people do display knowledge that is more consistent with other understandings of science. For example, their emphasis on practical problem solving is sometimes more consistent with pragmatism than it is with logical positivism. Even more plausibly, perhaps their naive assumptions about science have sociological rather than philosophical origins. Specifically, since World War II, modern science has marketed a highly idealized and naive image of itself to the public and the government. In that image, science is nearly infallible, always progressing, yielding ever increasing returns for each dollar allocated, and successfully self-monitoring and self-correcting. It seems far more plausible to attribute naive assumptions about science to our marketing of this naive image than to some presumed causal connection with logical positivism.

Defining the problem as logical positivism causes another difficulty. The definition of the problem contains the definition of the solution. If the problem is logical positivism, then the solution is educating evaluators and clients about logical positivism and about why it is such a bad idea. But if the problem is the marketing of a naive image of science, the solution is educating evaluators and clients about how science really works, warts and all. Viewed this way, the choice is clear. Educating clients about philosophy is, with few exceptions, a waste of our time and theirs.

For all these reasons, it is time to take on more worthy opponents than logical positivism. Fortunately, we do not lack for pretenders to the throne—social constructionism, naturalistic inquiry, hermeneutics, pragmatism, postmodernism, and a host of others. Each has staked out its turf, claiming more or less boldly to be first in line for the throne. But none has won wide intellectual acceptance, and none is heir apparent. The reason is that, while each of them may look pretty good when compared with logical positivism, all have significant problems when we compare them with one another—comparison that most tend to avoid.

The key contention of the present chapter is that there is good reason for this state of affairs: The main lesson of the last fifty years of epistemological and methodological debate is that no theory and no method provide a firm foundation for our inquiries. Hence, our guiding strategy should be to define an approach to inquiry that takes exactly this lesson as its main premise. The present chapter outlines such a strategy—critical multiplism (Cook, 1985). This strategy provides broad and general advice about how we should approach inquiry and about how we should select tactics to implement each of the many tasks that we face during inquiry. Some of these tasks include choice of methods, so methods are a special case of scientific tactics, but, because these tasks also include such matters as choice of question and decisions about how to facilitate the use of results in policy-making, this chapter will also show how critical multiplism approaches choice of tactics for these tasks as well.

Failure of Tactic

To understand why any particular tactic must be partly inadequate, consider the following question: What would the perfect method be like? The perfect method would have the following characteristics: It would be so inexpensive that we could always afford it, even if our budget was small. It would be so robust that it could provide an exact answer to the question, even under circumstances that made it hard to implement. It would be so reliable that it yielded few if any systematic or random errors. It would be so feasible that any scientist could learn to use it quickly and accurately, and no scientist would be deterred from using it solely because it was too difficult. It would be so unobtrusive that it would not interfere with other tasks in the study by virtue of logical or logistical incompatibility. It would be so powerful that, when it was applied, everyone would concede the outcome. And finally, it would be so well conceived and justified that it would not become outdated as the result of subsequent developments that were more accurate or efficient.

Perfect methods or anything reasonably approximating them would be intrinsically attractive for many reasons. They would give us time in which to think creatively about solving scientific problems rather than obsessing about details of methodology. They would make science more efficient by providing quick and ready answers to practical problems in research design. And they would circumvent the need to learn about the wide array of methodological techniques that might otherwise be required across the many different situations that we face as researchers. In short, perfect methods would allow us to train scientists once and for all in how to do their work, so that they could get on with solving the important substantive problems that they faced without being troubled by questions of method.

But, of course, the search for perfect methods seems doomed to fail. A reasonable interpretation of the history of science is that we have yet to discover a single scientific method that has not proved to be flawed in some respect when compared with the criteria just outlined. This is true not only of social science but of the natural sciences as well. For example, perhaps the nearest thing to a perfect method ever invented was O. H. Lowry's method for protein measurement in biology (Lowry, Rosenbrough, Farr, and Randall, 1951). According to *Science Citation Index,* it was cited more than fifty thousand times between 1961 and 1975, five times more often than the second most-cited work (Garfield, 1979). Since the current best interpretation of citation counts (Garfield, 1979) is that they are generally acceptable measures of use, this high count clearly suggests that an enormous number of scientists have found Lowry's method to be the method of choice. But it has important flaws. The ideal protein measurement method would be optimally cheap, rapid, and accurate. Unfortunately, it is difficult to meet all three criteria at the same time. Tests that are rapid and accurate are expensive, tests that are cheap and accurate are slow, and tests that are cheap and rapid are inaccurate. Lowry's method comes closest of any method to being cheap, rapid, and accurate for protein measurement, which no doubt accounts for its ubiquity. But it, too, ultimately falls short. For example, it is not as accurate as other tests when protein concentrations are small, and more recently developed methods have to be substituted in this circumstance.

If Lowry's method is not perfect, then can any method hope to be perfect? Probably not. Hence, while science must always develop better methods, such development may never provide a complete solution to the problem that single approaches are imperfect. The fundamental problem is that all scientific tactics are imperfect, because that is an inevitable feature of the finity or boundedness of human knowledge and action.

Failure of Strategy

However, the problem of methodological and tactical bias would not be anywhere nearly as severe as it is if scientists did not tend to adopt a systematically biased subset of these methods. But they do, because, as Kuhn (1970) has pointed out, scientists are taught from paradigms that include advice about the kinds of questions that are proper and the kinds of methods that are to be preferred. Each paradigm systematically includes some methods and excludes others. The result is that systematic biases of omission and commission are passed on to each new generation of scientists. To oversimplify, psychologists paradigmatically tend to prefer experimental methods and individual explanations of behavior, economists lean toward econometric models and profit maximization explanations, anthropologists sometimes gravitate toward case study and participant observation methods to construct a thick description of the case, and sociologists gravitate toward sociostructural explanations of phenomena. Compounding the problem, the social processes involved in teaching these paradigmatic strategies to novice scientists are more likely to exaggerate their superiority than they are to stress their strategic limitations. Consequently, we can expect that scientists will have significant difficulty conceptualizing their disciplinary strategies as biased rather than as best.

To some degree, of course, the narrowness of such paradigms reflects the fact that they are rightly tailored to the specific needs of the substantive area under study. For example, the double-blind, randomized clinical trial in medicine is a legitimate response to the needs of that field for answers about such questions as pharmaceutical efficacy. It is equally clear, however, that other paradigmatic methods are often unduly narrow or even misguided. For example, some psychologists rather mindlessly use some of the poorer quasi-experimental designs they learned in graduate school when the causal modeling techniques of sociologists or econometricians might be a more useful approach—or when causal questions should be abandoned entirely. Such problems, of course, become particularly acute when disciplinary paradigms are transferred en masse to interdisciplinary problems like program evaluation, where they are less clearly an appropriate response.

For all these reasons and others, scientists who rely on disciplinary training for scientific strategy are bound to produce research that is biased by paradigmatic errors of omission and commission. If so, then one of the more pressing needs in science is for the development of strategies that can uncover the biases of omission and commission that are inevitably present in all scientific methods and then ensure that they do not operate in the same direction in a study or in a research literature to yield a biased conclusion.

Critical Multiplism as a Research Strategy

Critical multiplism is a research strategy aimed at doing just that: It advises scientists to put together packages of imperfect methods and theories in a manner that minimizes constant biases (Cook, 1985; Houts, Cook, and Shadish, 1986; Shadish, 1986; Shadish, Cook, and Houts, 1986). Briefly, *multiplism* refers to the fact that any task in science can usually be conducted in any one of several ways, but in many cases no single way is known to be uniformly best. Under such circumstances, a multiplist advocates making heterogeneous those aspects of research about which uncertainty exists, so that the task is conducted in several different ways, each of which is subject to different biases. *Critical* refers to rational, empirical, and social efforts to identify the assumptions and biases present in the options chosen. Putting the two concepts together, we can say that the central tenet of critical multiplism is this: When it is not clear which of several defensible options for a scientific task is least biased, we should select more than one, so that our options reflect different biases, avoid constant biases, and leave no plausible bias overlooked. That multiple options yield similar results across operationalizations with different biases increases our confidence in the resulting knowledge. If different results occur when we do the task in different ways, then we have an empirical and conceptual problem to solve if we are to explain why this happened, but we are saved from a premature conclusion that a particular piece of knowledge is plausible.

Campbell and Fiske's (1959) multiple operationalism in measurement is the most widely known and appreciated form of multiplism. Its justification is prototypical of all multiplism, so it is instructive to review it here briefly. Any single measure contains bias of different sorts. For example, different investigators disagree about how a construct ought to be operationalized, and any single measure will undoubtedly reflect the preferences idiosyncratic to a small subset of all the investigators. Moreover, any single measure will contain some random error variance, some variance associated with the construct of interest, and some unique variance that is not related to the construct of interest but that is also not distributed randomly. Hence, no single measure is ever a perfect representation of a construct. Use of multiple measures helps investigators to note agreements and disagreements about how something ought to be measured, to note discrepancies in findings that vary as a function of presumptively significant differences among measures, and to compensate for the error and variance unique to any particular operationalization.

The move from multiple operationalism to critical multiplism is motivated partly by the observation that there is no logical reason for limiting it to measurement. Just as no single measure is perfect, no single approach to other tasks in science is without bias. Therefore, we may fruitfully explore the hypothesis that the same rationales that apply to multiple operationalism in measurement apply to the conduct of all tasks in science. That is, it might apply to question formation, where any single question is just one of many more or less important questions about a research problem, and no one question is always the right one to ask; theory or model selection, where any theory or model contains biases of omission and commission that make it at least partly incomplete or wrong; research design, where no research design is always optimal for answering a question, and under the best of circumstances each design feature clarifies different parts of a question; data analysis, where any particular way of analyzing data gives us an only partially complete picture of the results; interpretation of results, where many interpretations of the results of research will often have some validity; summarizing literatures, where we can never totally trust the results of a single study, but the aggregated results of multiple studies offer us an opportunity to explore how results vary over different ways of looking at a question; and research utilization, where no single method can ensure that the results of research will be useful or used either by other scientists or by the community that shapes policy. Each of these propositions represents a specific instance of the general strategy represented by critical multiplism: Always seek alternatives that can shed a different light on the problem.

Guidelines for Critical Multiplists

If I were to list guidelines for an approach to research from the critical multiplist perspective, I would have to formulate two kinds of guidelines: technical guidelines and social guidelines. Both kinds of guidelines would apply to all seven tasks outlined in the preceding paragraph.

    Technical Guidelines for Critical Multiplism. The first kind of guideline is technical. There are seven technical guidelines:

1. Identify the tasks to be done.
2. Identify different options for doing each task.
3. Identify the strengths, biases, and assumptions associated with each option.
4. When it is not clear which of several defensible options for doing a task

is least biased, select more than one to reflect different biases, avoid constant biases, and overlook only the least plausible biases.
5. Note convergences of results over options with different biases.
6. Explain differences of results yielded by options with different biases.
7. Publicly defend any decisions to leave a task homogeneous.

The technical tasks specified by these guidelines aim at creating heterogeneous biases in planned research and identifying the biases that were and were not present in completed research.

We can illustrate these guidelines first with an example from basic research in psychology, then with one from applied research on the topic of AIDS. In the former case, personality theory has long discussed a controversy referred to as the *person-situation debate*. Essentially, it involves the extent to which individual behavior is influenced by person variables, such as personality traits, or by characteristics of the situation, or by some interaction between the two. Not too long ago, I and two colleagues applied critical multiplist guidelines to an analysis of the research bearing on that debate (Houts, Cook, and Shadish, 1986). We began with the premise that many options that might be studied were implicit in the question—many personality traits, many behaviors that might serve as dependent variables, many kinds of situations, and many data analytic strategies that might provide indexes of behavioral consistency. Various combinations of these options constituted different ways of framing the person-situation issue. Through a review of the literature, we were able to show that researchers in this area had examined a remarkably small combination of the possible questions that could have been asked. More important, individual researchers often framed the issue in different ways. When their research seemed to generate different results, it was often because they had asked systematically different versions of the question. In the few cases where they asked the same version of the question, they tended to get the same answer. Finally, we were also able to uncover some biases of commission in these studies, errors yielding results that were plausibly biased in the direction that we believed the authors to have preferred, given their theoretical predilections. I will return to this example often as this article proceeds in order to elaborate how critical multiplism can be applied.

Now consider an example from AIDS research, a pressing applied social research issue. Suppose that we wished to answer the following question: Are high-risk groups changing their behavior in a way that might minimize their likelihood of being infected? The next step, if we follow critical multiplist guidelines, is to identify the options for answering this question, options that might plausibly result in different answers, and then try to ensure that no important option has been systematically overlooked in the literature as a whole. The answer to the question may depend, for example, on the group that we elect to study: homosexuals, intravenous drug users, or hemophiliacs. If we are studying a treatment, the answer may depend on whether that treatment is administered in individual counseling or to a group of peers in which peer pressure can be brought to bear, or it may depend on whether treatment is administered by health professionals or by community organizations that historically have access to and credibility with the target population. The answer may also depend on the dependent variables that we elect to examine: knowledge of AIDS risks, actual safe-sex practices, sharing of needles, or promiscuous heterosexual contact. It may depend on whether we assess the occurrence of these behaviors by simple self-report, by observing behavior where feasible, by assessing gonorrhea infections and hepatitis as proxies for the likelihood of AIDS infection, or by trying random response techniques. It may depend on whether we collect these dependent variables in the long term or the short term, or cross-sectionally or longitudinally, and on whether we have a federal certificate of confidentiality with which we can at least try to reassure respondents. Finally, it may depend on whether we conduct the study in San Francisco, Indianapolis, or Nigeria. All possible combinations of these options suggest the universe of studies that could be conducted to answer this question. Clearly, no single one of these versions of the question is the correct one, so our research strategy should be to ensure that we have overlooked no plausible version of the question unless we can make a good case that it would not yield results different from the research that has already been done. Undoubtedly, a review of the AIDS literature would reveal that some of these versions of the question had been studied extensively, while others had not been studied at all, and that the answer to the question is positive in some versions but negative in others. Organizing such a review around these multiple options would point to future studies that seem important to do but that have not yet been done, and it would force us to try to explain why the answers to the question vary depending on how the question is operationalized.

This example is not meant to imply that critical multiplism limits itself to options for formulating good research questions. It is much broader than that. In the example just given, we could have focused on design options for answering a treatment outcome study based on this question. We could have focused on options for estimating whether the results of the study would generalize to the population of high-risk persons in the United States. We could even have focused on whether this question was worth asking at all given other competing questions that could be asked about, say, the prevalence of seropositivity or the costs of AIDS. In all these matters, there will be different ways of proceeding—different designs, analyses, and questions to ask—all of which we need to consider carefully before we draw conclusions about AIDS that might be premature until the complete set of options has been thoughtfully considered.

Being Multiplist with Limited Resources. Resource constraints usually prevent us from including all the heterogeneous options that our analysis suggests are warranted. Hence, we must often decide what to make multiple in a particular study. The following corollary guidelines can help us to make the choice:

1. Include only the options that can be defended as presumptively likely to yield different results.
2. Give preference to options that have been left homogeneous in past studies.
3. Decide how much uncertainty reduction is desired or needed given the situation, and then select options that might be able to provide that level.
4. Select options that are financially feasible in the context of the study. Use the following rough guides to help conceptualize the costs of making different options heterogeneous: The least expensive options include multiple measures on the same subjects, multiple data analyses by the same investigator with different models and assumptions, and the submission of research proposals and reports to multiple critics. The moderately expensive options involve multiple kinds of subjects, observers, and occasions; multiple analyses of the same data set by different investigators; and the hiring of multiple consultants for on-site visits. The most expensive option is implementation by multiple independent investigators at different sites.
5. Publicly defend any decisions to leave a task homogeneous.

Particularly for options that are presumptively important in their implications for changing the results of a study, there is little excuse for not implementing at least the least expensive options for being multiplist.

Social Guidelines for Critical Multiplism. Critical multiplism requires the investigator to be aware of all the tasks that need to be done, the options for doing each task, and the biases and assumptions associated with each option. But individual scientists are limited in their capacity to know all these matters, they have difficulty perceiving their own biases, and they are insulated from obtaining some of the knowledge that they need by such sociological structures as academic disciplines (Faust, 1984; Mahoney, 1976). The problem is compounded because, as D'Espagnat (1983, p. 133) put it, "the human mind is spontaneously overconfident on such matters. In particular, it too frequently raises ideas that look 'clear and distinct' to the level of absolute truths. It sometimes fails to note the cases in which the notions in question are, in fact, of questionable validity or are relevant merely within some limited context."

For such reasons, we must expect that individual investigators will fail to complete the technical tasks of critical multiplism in a way that clearly identifies all the options and biases. Thus, we must have a second set of guidelines aimed at remedying the social and psychological limitations of individual investigators in accomplishing the technical component in a satisfactory manner:

1. Identify several sources (people, past research, competing theories) whose biases are likely to differ from those of the person who completed the technical tasks.
2. Enlist the aid of those sources in completing and criticizing the results of the technical component.

In AIDS research, for example, this social psychological component of critical multiplism could be implemented by seeking input from multiple groups that have an interest in AIDS so that we can be more confident that important perspectives and options have not been overlooked; commissioning multiple independent studies of the same question by different investigators around the nation, each of whom would be encouraged to communicate but to pursue independent investigations of the topic; submitting raw data from all these studies to multiple analysts, each of whom would use different assumptions and techniques to uncover biases of omission and commission; and sending the report of results to multiple interest groups who could point out hidden biases and assumptions in the study and its interpretation. In all these examples, a cardinal guideline is that criticism is fostered best when its source has a perspective that is quite different from that of the original investigator.

What Critical Multiplism Is Not. It might help us to clarify critical multiplism if we consider what it is not. The opposite of multiplism is monism—always doing some task in the same way. The opposite of being critical is to be mindless in the choices that one makes. Hence, the extreme opposite of critical multiplism is mindless monism—always doing things in the same way without thinking about the strengths and weaknesses of one's choices. This is probably more prevalent than we would like to think, partly because biases in disciplinary training tend to expose us to limited sets of options and partly because thinking critically about one's work is both intellectually and emotionally demanding. Nevertheless, being a mindless monist is probably not a good thing. It is a surefire way of getting into trouble, because good critics will eventually find the problems with your research unless you find them first.

However, we should also consider the other two possible options, mindless multiplism and critical monism, for they afford more interesting contrasts. Mindless multiplism is introducing some variation in options without really thinking much about it. My favorite example is most uses of stepwise multiple regression. Stepwise multiple regression throws multiple predictors into a regression; the computer selects the ones to enter into the equation. Very little in science is more mindless than this, and in general such work is to be discouraged. However, we might be willing to allow at least a minor place for truly mindless multiplism in research in the interests of generating diverse and unanticipated perspectives on a problem, much as Campbell (1974) called in his evolutionary epistemology for blind variations in the social problem-solving options that we choose to study. It might maximize the chance of encountering some truly novel solution to a problem. Problematically, Campbell's justification really requires the variations to be random, and mindlessness seldom achieves that goal, because its tendency is to fall back on habit. Habit is not random.

However, there is a place in research for critical monism—doing many things in the same way even though one has thought critically about the possible weaknesses of doing so. The tendency toward critical monism results from the fact that our time, skills, and resources are limited, so we can only implement one or at most a few options in any given study. Still, examining the strengths and weaknesses of the options that you do choose critically will help you both to choose the best option for your study and to anticipate valid criticisms of the options that you have chosen so you can qualify your conclusions accordingly. Hence, it is more realistic to strive for some mixture of critical monism and critical multiplism in one's research. I discuss these practical matters again at the end of this chapter.

Applications of Critical Multiplism

Earlier, I listed seven tasks that scientists must address: question formation, theory or model selection, research design, data analysis, interpretation of results, summarizing literatures, and research utilization. The examples in this section show how critical multiplism can be applied to each of these tasks.

Critical Multiplism and Question Formation. Here, the critical multiplist searches for constant biases in the kinds of questions that have and have not been asked and for bias in the way in which past research has operationalized questions. Critical multiplism in question formation is particularly important because the questions that scientists ask implicitly contain both a conceptualization of the problem that they are addressing and the seeds of actions that might be taken to remedy the problem (Rein and Schon, 1977). Thus, without critical scrutiny of these questions, scientists risk a wrong or biased conceptualization of the problem and consequent ineffective or insufficiently limited action. Unfortunately, we probably know less about how scientists formulate their questions than about any other aspect of their behavior. This omission is probably all the more unfortunate since the value of research may depend more on the value of the question being investigated than on any other single factor, because the value of the enterprise as a whole can be compromised from the start by investigating the wrong question. Playing on statistical terminology describing Type I and Type II errors in testing the null hypothesis, Dunn (1982) refers to this problem as *making Type III errors*—setting confidence intervals correctly when testing null hypotheses about the wrong problem.

However, in critical multiplist terms, the problem is not one of simply asking either the right or the wrong question. Rather, it is that we should be wary, either as individual researchers or across a field as a whole, of asking a possibly good set of questions that nonetheless systematically shapes the issues in a biased manner. Thus, we should carefully scrutinize and criticize our questions on two levels. The first level concerns the general kinds of questions that we are and are not asking. For instance, in the early part of this decade, federal agencies seemed to be reluctant to fund AIDS research that dealt with the question of safe sex. I know of one research team whose grant proposal on that topic had conveniently been lost by the agency for a prolonged period of time. The investigators were eventually given an indirect message that such research was not being encouraged because it implicitly condoned homosexual behavior, which was not consistent with the political climate then current at the federal level. Fortunately, this grant proposal was eventually found and later funded, speaking either to the power of a life-threatening crisis to influence the political process or, as one observer put it, to the more mundane but equally powerful influence of the condom lobby, given the profits that it might make if some safe-sex habits were adopted (Turner, 1988). If nothing else, this example underlines the extent to which question formation is a social, political, and economic process and so must be critically analyzed as such.

But we should be more worried about instances of biased question formation that are less obvious than the example just given. A colleague of mine suggested that we should be studying the long-term social psychological impacts of AIDS on how we relate to one another in American society. His concern stemmed from a conversation with his eight-year-old daughter, who came home from school discussing not only the explicit details of sexual activity but also her fears of such activities, since they might ultimately have fatal consequences. She had not learned all this from any AIDS education classes, since such classes had not yet been implemented in the public school system that she attended. Rather she gleaned most of it from her peers—eloquent testimony to the way in which social and sexual norms are being challenged and shaped among young children. We may be living with this consequence of the AIDS epidemic long after we have achieved some success in limiting its physical consequences.

Another example of a gap in the kinds of questions that we ask about AIDS concerns women and AIDS. Probably largely because women account for such a small percentage of AIDS cases, we have very little data on such matters as female sexual behaviors regarding AIDS or the course of the disease in women. But looking down the road ten years, we may regret this omission if AIDS spreads increasingly to the heterosexual community, if we begin to be more concerned about the spread of AIDS among prostitutes, or if the issue of abortion rights confronts the issue of bearing babies with AIDS.

Once we have decided to ask a particular kind of question, there are still several different ways of asking the question that might plausibly yield different results. We have already examined the many different ways in which we can address the question of whether high-risk groups are changing their behavior. Another example comes from the colleague who works on the aforementioned safe-sex study. In tracing the epidemiology of homosexual behaviors so as to help identify safe-sex practices, the investigators in that project made the initially plausible assumption that an increasing number of sexual partners was the key factor in becoming infected. Therefore, they neglected to ask about the number of encounters with each partner, a variable that later research proved to be an important factor. Significantly, colleagues at the same institution had already determined that the number of encounters was important, but my colleague's team did not discover this owing to the lack of communication across teams at the institution—a point that underscores why the social psychological component of critical multiplism is so important.

Another example concerns the examination by Houts, Cook, and Shadish (1986) of the person-situation debate. That topic had been marked by decades of controversy and seemingly contradictory research about whether personality traits, situational constraints, or some interaction between person and situation best predicted behavior both within and across occasions and settings. Yet our analysis showed that many of the differences among authors resulted from the fact that they were asking quite different versions of the same question. The most important source of difference between thinkers concerns their sampling of traits, behaviors, settings, and occasions. Epstein (1979) used multiple behaviors reported over multiple occasions to examine multiple traits, but the behaviors often occurred in a single setting or in multiple settings that could be unconfounded with occasions. Hence, Mischel and Peake (1982) considered his work to have limited relevance for the issue of transsituational stability. Buss and Craik (1983) dealt with multiple settings, multiple traits, and multiple behaviors within each trait category. However, their work is less relevant to concerns about the situational stability of a particular discrete behavior (behavioral consistency) than it is to concerns about dispositions defined as measures of different behaviors presumed to belong to the same latent trait (dispositional consistency). Both Bem and Allen (1974) and Mischel and Peake (1982) examined two traits, multiple behaviors within each trait, multiple settings, and multiple occasions.

However, Bem and Allen (1974) do this in an idiographic mode, so that only Mischel and Peake (1982) have independently sampled traits, behaviors, settings, and times in the nomothetic mode in which the person-situation debate has been mostly pursued. Sampling has to occur within each of the four factors if analysts are to explore the stability of behaviors across settings, especially when the behaviors are presumed to represent a trait, and we want to develop theory that is not specific to a few idiosyncratically selected traits. It follows that the person-situation debate has rarely been about the same questions, so that much of the disagreement has been about defining the question, not necessarily about the answer to the question that has been posed.

Critical Multiplism and Theory or Model Selection. Here, the task is to ensure that inadvertent constant biases have not crept into our selection of the theories and models that we use to conceptualize a problem and guide our research on it. Any theory or model contains biases of omission and commission that make it at least partly incomplete or wrong. This statement is true even in the most well-developed physical sciences. For example, the theory of quantum mechanics applied to particle physics may be the single most successful theory in the history of science, because it integrates and explains an enormous array of diverse observations. Yet even here, physicists and philosophers disagree about how to explain certain experimental phenomena that seem to imply a counterintuitive nonseparability of distant particles (D'Espagnat, 1983; Rae, 1986). The interviews with physicists involved in this controversy presented in a recent, highly accessible book (Davies and Brown, 1986) make it clear that they propose radically different and inconsistent explanations of the problem, none of which seems to be completely successful. In the social and medical sciences, of course, we lack theories or models as well developed as quantum mechanics. But there are still plenty of examples that point vividly to the need to retain and consider multiple theories and models. For example, in learning theory in the 1950s, Spence and Tolman debated the role of cognition in learning, with Tolman's position receiving significant vindication only twenty years after the debate was thought to have been resolved in Spence's favor (Gholson and Barker, 1985). In the medical sciences, many molecular biologists and geneticists rejected Barbara McClintock's work on mobile genetic elements because it was inconsistent with constancy of the genome, the dogma that prevailed at the time (Keller, 1983; Lewin, 1983). Rejected theories and models have a way of coming back to haunt us in newer, better-supported forms that force us to revise our theories and models once again. Disconcertingly, these matters are seldom superficially clear, and it is rarely that one theory is widely thought to be best even for a short time. Far more often, theories and models contend actively, each backed by a group of scientists that fervently argues on behalf of its pet approach.

Since AIDS research is a relatively new endeavor, it is even more apparent that we are still groping to locate the best theories and models for it. It is probably fair to say that we view AIDS mostly as a medical and psychological problem, so we apply available medical and psychological theories and models to it. Just as it is true that the way in which we frame questions shapes the actions that we later recommend, so it is true that the theories we bring to bear shape the actions that we take. If we view AIDS as a medical problem, we recommend medical and public health solutions. If we view it as a psychological problem, we see the solution as lying in changed attitudes and behaviors. Other theoretical perspectives on AIDS are far less common. But perhaps we should consider them as well. For example, blacks and Hispanics account for about 40 percent of the men with AIDS, although together they represent only about 17 percent of the population. The overwhelming majority of women and children with AIDS are members of minority groups. If we explore this overrepresentation of minorities, we might well find that economic and social causes are as critical or more critical than biological and psychological ones. That is, it may be that AIDS is more prevalent in these populations than in others for the same economic and social factors that contribute to drug abuse, prostitution, and other phenomena observed in the underclass. If so, we would be led to consider social and economic solutions to the problem. Of course, critical analysis might then lead us to conclude that we cannot do much about the root social and economic causes of drug abuse or prostitution and that it is therefore more feasible to implement discrete behavioral solutions, such as distributing clean needles. But we cannot do this critical analysis until we have at least considered some alternative conceptualizations of the problem. And in the years to come, if medical and behavioral solutions seem insufficient to cope with AIDS, we may be forced to reconsider some social and economic interventions.

Metatheoretical differences also had an effect on the evolution of the person-situation debate. Some researchers—especially Bem (1983)—preferred an idiographic approach that left subjects free to define which behaviors represented which traits. Others—especially Epstein (1979)—operated within a more traditional nomothetic conception that defined traits uniformly over people. Still others—especially Mischel (1979)—operated within a more social-cognitive theory that replaced traits with information-processing concepts or—like Buss and Craik (1984) in particular—operated within a theory of personality that conceptualized traits only in terms of overt behaviors assumed to indicate common latent traits. These metatheoretical differences led each thinker to formulate and study different questions, as we saw in the preceding section.

Critical Multiplism and Research Design. In designing research, we often find that we could use any of several different methods to construct an answer. When many different options have been used to study a problem and when they all converge on the same result, we are tempted to be confident in the result. But such confidence is misplaced if all these methods nonetheless still share a common bias. One example concerns evaluations of federal social programs aimed at improving pregnancy outcome—such programs as the Maternal and Child Health Program (MCH) or the Special Supplemental Food Program for Women, Infants, and Children (WIC). One review that examined about thirty such evaluations (Shadish and Reis, 1984) found that the studies used a wide array of methods, including surveys, one-group pretest-posttest designs, regression modeling, and time series. Across these different methods, the result was largely the same, namely that the programs improved pregnancy outcomes. Yet despite the apparent diversity of method, the studies all shared a common bias. That is, almost none of the studies reported whether the mother had received treatment from a program other than the program under review, although it seemed quite likely that mothers were receiving additional services, since there are more than seventy federal programs that can seemingly have an impact on pregnancy outcomes. In fact, the one study that did document mothers who had received other treatment (Sharpe and Wetherbee, 1980) found that the addition of WIC services to the other treatment had no beneficial effects.

For an example from AIDS research, we can examine models of the spread of the HIV infection. Turner, Fay, and Widdus (1988) reviewed three different models of this problem that yielded estimates ranging between 750,000 and 2.5 million infected persons. The models were multiplist in the sense that each model used different assumptions, different sources of data, and different statistical procedures. Turner, Fay, and Widdus (1988) added a commendably critical analysis of these different models, locating significant sources of uncertainty in each. Thus, they pointed out that one model depended on a fraction that changes substantially as an epidemic progresses, so that estimates from a patient population in which the virus has only recently been introduced will differ substantially from estimates for populations in which the virus has only recently appeared. Another method used estimates of the number of homosexual males in the United States compiled in the 1940s by Kinsey, Pomeroy, and Martin (1948) from data gathered among college-educated people in the midwest—data whose relevance to today's problem is doubtful.

But from a critical multiplist perspective, the analysis just reviewed still lacks one important feature. In all their otherwise excellent discussion, the authors did not attempt to estimate the direction of the biases introduced by these uncertainties. For example, experts in the field undoubtedly have some knowledge of whether the Kinsey data over- or underestimate the prevalence of homosexuality among American males today. Armed with such knowledge, we would then be in a better position to judge whether the 1986 estimates produced by the U.S. Public Health

Service were likely to over- or underestimate the number of persons infected with the HIV virus. More generally, if we could determine the likely direction of bias in each of the three models, we would be closer to understanding the accuracy of current estimates.

Dawes (1989) suggests a somewhat different example in his discussion of rating scale methods of assessing the risk of various behaviors that can lead to AIDS. He points out that all the questions on the AIDS knowledge and attitude surveys conducted by the National Center for Health Statistics (NCHS) use traditional normative rating scale response formats. In fact, every such survey ever done on this topic uses normative rather than ipsative formats (Turner, 1988). Dawes (1989) points out that the ambiguity in such rating scales makes it very unclear exactly how risky the public understands these behaviors to be, especially relative to one another. He suggests an alternative ipsative methodology, ranking or paired comparisons techniques, that would eliminate much of this ambiguity and thus yield more accurate assessments of our understanding of the relative riskiness of various behaviors.

To turn again to the person-situation debate (Houts, Cook, and Shadish, 1986), method selection among the many researchers evolved naturally to include at least some multiplism. Over studies and less rarely within studies, researchers have examined multiple personality traits, multiple situations, multiple occasions, and multiple criterion behaviors. But this evolution was haphazard at best, and there was little careful thought about how one could best sample multiple options with each of these four categories. For example, selection of traits was guided more by convenience and prior substantive interest than by a theoretical analysis of traits in general or of the types of traits that might be more or less consistent across situations. The same thing can be said for sampling of situations, sampling of behaviors, and the time frames under which cross-situational consistency could be expected to be observed. Consequently, the findings that accumulated were of quite uncertain generalizability. Perhaps most seriously, when the major research question is one about behavioral stability across situations, it is crucial to examine the same behavior in different settings, yet none of the studies examined did any systematic unconfounding of situation with behavior. As a result, the key question of cross-situational consistency remained quite open.

Critical Multiplism and Data Analysis. To begin with, a healthy dose of exploratory data analysis has no equal for creating heterogeneity of perspective (Tukey, 1977). Moreover, for almost every data set, there are several analytic methods that could be used to answer a question. Sometimes there is evidence that one analytic technique is probably superior to others, as when modern linear structural modeling techniques replace analysis of covariance (ANCOVA) to adjust for group nonequivalence given the problems that ANCOVA incurs as the result of unreliable measurement (Cook and Campbell, 1979). Often there is doubt that one analytic technique is best, in which case more than one technique ought to be used so that we can see whether varying our analytic methods causes our results to vary. In such cases, we can test competing causal models, as several authors did with the Head Start quasi-experimental outcome data (Cicirelli and Associates, 1969; Magidson, 1977; Rindskopf, 1981). Rossi, Berk, and Lenihan (1980) provide another example. In analyzing data from a randomized experiment, they used both traditional analysis of variance that tested the direct effects of treatment and three-stage least squares to investigate some mediating processes. In each of these cases, more was learned from the joint use of multiple analyses than from any single analysis in isolation.

For an example in AIDS research, we can look at a recent protocol from the Agency for Health Care Policy and Research (AHCPR) projecting the number and cost of future AIDS cases as a function of the many variables over which the estimate could change. The AHCPR notes that such variables include the extent of seropositivity in different areas of the country, the probability of HIV infection associated with different modes of transmission, specific cofactors that can increase the likelihood of transmission for a given individual, the duration of the incubation period, and a patient's expected life span after acquiring ARC or AIDS. The AHCPR protocol calls for flexible mathematical models incorporating these key parameters that permit us to perform sensitivity analyses in order to determine the parameters that contribute most to the uncertainty of future projections. Thompson and Meyer (1989), using different assumptions about parameters that might affect estimates of the costs of AIDS, advocate similar sensitivity analyses, and Lagakos (1989) suggests that survival analysis can be used to give a range of plausible estimates that realistically portray the uncertainties encountered in understanding the course of AIDS.

The analysis of the person-situation debate by Houts, Cook, and Shadish (1986) provides another example of critical multiplism in data analysis. There, we reanalyzed a data set that Mischel and Peake (1982) had published. We were guided by the hypothesis that several biases in the data may have led those authors systematically to underestimate the overall cross-situational consistency in behavior: The reliability of the items measuring traits was generally quite low, which would attenuate correlations. The reliability of behaviors was also low. The authors had not used a Fisher z-transformation in cumulating correlations (while this transformation is controversial, its use would have increased correlations even further). Moreover, we had reason to think that item distributions might have been skewed or restricted in range, which would further lower correlations. Finally, the procedures that the authors had used to average over items may have underestimated cross-situational consistency because the items may not have all been good measures of the same core construct. While our reanalysis could not remedy all these problems, the corrections that we could apply indeed supported the suspicion that problems in the original analysis may have systematically underestimated cross-situational consistency. This case shows that multiple analytic options can lead to biases that all run in a constant direction.

Critical Multiplism and Interpretation of Results. The goal in applying critical multiplism to the interpretation of research results is first to generate an array of possible interpretations, then to assess those interpretations as either more or less plausible on the basis of available evidence. In AIDS research, a particularly ingenious example was provided by Valdiserri and others (1988), who were concerned with interpreting the fact that the HIV virus can be recovered from saliva (Groopman and others, 1984). Some might interpret this finding to mean that intimate kissing is not a safe sexual practice, since the virus could be transmitted through exchange of saliva. But by bringing in multiple lines of evidence that provided new information from different perspectives, Valdiserri and others (1988) developed another interpretation. That is, since recovery of the HIV virus from saliva has been shown to be far less frequent than its recovery from blood (Ho and others, 1985), intimate kissing is less likely than other sexual activities to be a likely route of transmission. Findings from studies of a related infection support this hypothesis. That is, it has been shown that oral-oral contact is not related to seropositivity for the hepatitis B virus although that virus is found in saliva (Schreeder and others, 1982). While there was probably still some possibility of transmission through intimate kissing, Valdiserri and others (1988) interpreted this marginal possibility as allowing intimate kissing to be classified as a "possibly safe-sex" practice.

We see another example in the reanalysis by Houts, Cook, and Shadish (1986) of the Mischel and Peake (1982) data on the person-situation debate. Mischel and Peake (1982) asked whether the trait of conscientiousness predicted cross-situational consistency. Somewhat haphazard procedures and criteria had been used to generate the items pertaining to conscientiousness. Consequently, different observers could have different opinions about the items that were appropriate measures of the trait. Hence, we used only the items that subjects considered to be most typical of conscientiousness, and the results again suggested more cross-situational consistency than the original authors had reported. Differences in interpretation about what counts as conscientiousness thus lead to differences in conclusions about the stability of behavior.

More generally, we suggested that the results of research on the person-situation debate could be interpreted from the vantage point of similar work in social psychology on the relations between attitudes and behaviors. This area, like the other, has generated large amounts of research and controversy, and researchers in both areas have spent a great deal of time trying to agree on estimations of the magnitude of the relationships between traits and behavior on the one hand and between attitudes and behavior on the other. Yet the literature on attitudes and behaviors moved much more rapidly to address two other kinds of questions: questions about the contingencies that govern variation in magnitude and questions about the mechanisms through which behaviors express general attitudes in specific situations. This clearly pointed to a gap in the person-situation literature and allowed us to describe an extensive program of research that might help fill it.

Critical Multiplism and Single Studies. For all the reasons discussed on the preceding pages, we can never totally trust the results of a single study. So if a single study reports that HIV-infected teenagers developed AIDS more slowly than either infants or adults, we are best advised to note the finding but view it with suspicion. But when several studies conducted by independent investigators in different cities all report the same finding, we should note the convergence of results. Even so, we should still look for constant biases that might plausibly account for the finding. Indeed, all three studies had a constant bias—all were conducted with hemophiliac teenagers. While we have no reason to believe that AIDS progresses differently in the presence of hemophilia, it may be that the longer latency observed in these studies is nonetheless an artifact of the fact that hemophiliacs as a group may have been infected with HIV somewhat more recently (for example, 1982–1984) than homosexuals (1978–1980), given that some time is bound to have elapsed between the initial appearance of the virus and contamination of the blood supply used by hemophiliacs. Unfortunately, this is one case that gets more rather than less complicated as multiple lines of evidence are brought to bear. That is, other lines of evidence support the finding that children may develop some diseases more slowly or less severely—chickenpox or measles, for example.

In AIDS research, Turner (1988) analyzed public perceptions and behavior in response to AIDS by examining, searching for convergences and divergences, and in some cases reanalyzing data from four different national surveys. Thus, he found that public fear of AIDS varied as the result of how the question was asked. Between 17 and 28 percent of the respondents answered in the affirmative when they were asked whether they were afraid or concerned about contracting AIDS, but only 10 percent—about half as many—said they felt that they were at risk of contracting AIDS. Similar variations were found in public attitudes about quarantine for AIDS victims, with only 17 percent saying that they should be quarantined as lepers are but with 51 percent agreeing that AIDS should be added to the list of diseases that must be quarantined. We can almost always learn more from a critical analysis of multiple studies than we can from examination of the results of a single study.

The analysis of the person-situation debate by Houts, Cook, and Shadish (1986) reflects the same principle. It was the contrast among the many studies that we reviewed that caused us to appreciate the variety of dimensions on which the studies differed—traits, behaviors, situations, and occasions, to name only a few. With this larger perspective, we could then see the gaps in each individual study, which in turn led us to guide our reanalysis of the Mischel and Peake (1982) data partly by trying to study those gaps. But by cumulating studies, we could also examine the findings that were common despite the fact that the individual studies were so different in so many ways. For example, studies generally agreed that personality tests are of little use in making predictions about single behaviors in specific situations and that there was strong evidence for the temporal stability of behavior within situations.

Critical Multiplism and Research Utilization. No single method will suffice to ensure that the results of research will be useful or used, either by other scientists or by the community that shapes policy. Those involved in applied social and medical research learned this lesson the hard way over the last twenty years (Shadish, Cook, and Leviton, 1991). From simple reliance on such traditional techniques of dissemination as publication and presentation at conventions, scientists who want their work to be used have added to their repertoire such techniques as preparing executive summaries outlining major findings and recommendations in simple terms, consulting with users before starting the research to learn what kinds of information they want and might be able to use, keeping in close contact with users during the course of the study, providing interim results prior to the final report, and making use of media presentations in such forms as news conferences and press releases.

By virtue of their training and socialization, however, most scientists probably avoid most of the techniques just identified except those tied to publication and interaction with peers. AIDS research is probably somewhat of an exception to this rule, given the extent of public concern about the problems involved. Media attention has been forced on many AIDS researchers, and especially at the federal level, the nature of federal funding for AIDS research tends to focus researchers' attention on gathering data that federal agencies see as holding the most promise for immediate use. But we might still wonder what kinds of biases have crept into our conceptions of useful AIDS research. While I am generally not familiar enough with AIDS research to answer this question with certainty, I can say that I would ask two questions about this matter. The first concerns biases in the selection of stakeholder groups—the groups that, directly or indirectly, are affected by AIDS and AIDS research—whose input has helped to shape the kinds of information that AIDS researchers have gathered. We have probably done a good job of gathering data that might be useful to the general medical and public health community and to the federal agencies most directly concerned with treatment for AIDS patients and paying for AIDS treatments. But it is not clear that we are trying as hard to provide useful information to the dying AIDS patient who wants to know where and how he can most comfortably live out his remaining time in dignity, to the local school superintendent who wants to know how to convince angry parents that it is in the community's best interests to educate their children about AIDS, or to the families of hemophiliac children who do not know how to cope with their child's illness and who see AIDS destroying their hopes, dreams, and finances.

The second question that I would ask concerns the distinction between short-term and long-term use. For very understandable reasons, AIDS research has adopted a crisis mentality, with nearly all the federal AIDS dollars going into research aimed at coping with the immediate impacts of the AIDS crisis. But there is another kind of use that we should also be thinking of, a kind of long-term use aimed at enlightening us about the full scope of the AIDS problem in all its ramifications and about the long-term impacts and changes that it may have on American society. What, for example, would John Naisbitt, author of *Megatrends* (Naisbitt, 1984), say about the way in which AIDS will transform our lives? This kind of research, broader and perhaps more exploratory in scope than research aimed at solving more immediate concerns, is nonetheless just as essential to our long-term ability to cope with AIDS.

Invalid Objections to Critical Multiplism

Some readers might raise three objections to critical multiplism: First, there really are methods in science that are uniformly acknowledged to be superior—for instance, the randomized experiment and the random sample survey in social and medical research. As a result, critical multiplism is misguided and even misleading in suggesting otherwise. Second, the tenets of critical multiplism cannot be true because, when we apply them reflexively to critical multiplism itself, they imply that it, too, is imperfect and cannot lay claim to being the right approach to inquiry. Third, critical multiplism implicitly approves the notion that anything goes and considers all methods, practices, and interpretations to be equally valid. None of these objections is accurate. But let us consider each of them in turn.

Random Assignment and Sampling as Ideal Methods. Most readers need no introduction to the ideas of random sampling from populations and of random assignment to experimental conditions. Both ideas have a long and illustrious career in science (Campbell and Stanley, 1963; Fisher, 1925; Rossi, Wright, and Anderson, 1983). Random sampling helps enormously with generalization from samples to the populations from which the samples have been drawn, and random assignment to conditions greatly facilitates causal inferences. There can be no question that these are two of the most useful methodological tools in the social scientist's repertoire.

The first thing to note, however, is that both techniques are in fact multiplist. Recall that multiplism aims to make heterogeneous those aspects of research that might bias results. The aim is to leave no systematic bias dominant in the results. In principle, both random assignment and random sampling accomplish exactly this with regard to the unit of assignment or sampling, making it likely within a known probability that no systematic biases are present either among units in the sample or across groups. In research where the sampling unit is a person, as is often the case in social science and medical research, this amounts to treating people as a facet of the research design and making subjects heterogeneous so that they do not share any irrelevant characteristic that might be confounded with the desired inference. Random procedures are therefore the most plausible ways of accomplishing the goals of multiplism, especially because they can be taught routinely to scientists and implemented robustly in research.

This point underscores that the key guideline of critical multiplism is not that multiple options should always be implemented. Rather, the key guideline is hedged by the condition *when it is not clear which of several defensible options for a scientific task is least biased.* Only then should multiple options with divergent biases be selected. It is sometimes the case that an option is in fact quite plausibly the least biased of several options that could be implemented. Since that will often be the case for random procedures, they will often be the method of choice.

But for many reasons we are likely to overestimate the value of random procedures and to place confidence in them in situations where it is not warranted. Our overconfidence is probably rooted in the social and psychological processes involved in teaching the techniques to novice scientists during their initial disciplinary training. Because we want to encourage new scientists to think routinely about such methods and because time limits what a single course during graduate school can cover, we often simplify the presentation of random techniques and put off discussions of their weaknesses and vulnerable assumptions to a later date. However, this later date often never arrives, so that scientists then tend to use these methods in rote fashion without much further thought. After all, the pressures of a research career often make us reluctant to take time to reflect on possible flaws in the methods that we habitually use or to learn new techniques that are both conceptually and methodologically difficult. Under these circumstances, routine reliance on random procedures may not be such a bad thing if it serves to ensure that many scientists are using methods that, on the whole, are among the best we have.

Nonetheless, criticizing random procedures reminds us of their many limitations and encourages us to think of alternatives in the many situations in which random procedures are not the best choice. To begin with, random procedures work well only if certain assumptions are met. When those assumptions are not met, as they often are not, random procedures must be complemented or even replaced by other methods. For example, consider random assignment to conditions. Chen and Rossi (1987) claim that random assignment to conditions facilitates causal inference only to the extent that the sample is large, or the sample is homogeneous, or the experiment has been repeated many times; there are no interactions between treatment variables and extraneous variables; attrition rates are the same among experimentals and controls; and conditioning variables affect all important subdivisions of the experiment evenly.

Many of these same assumptions, or variables on them, also apply to random sampling. Thus, Cook and Campbell (1979) point out that random assignment to conditions does not control for the problems in causal inference that occur when treatment intended for one group is communicated to another group (treatment diffusion), when program administrators cannot tolerate the focused inequality that results from restricting treatment to some subjects and so offer compensatory treatment to subjects in control or less-desirable-treatment groups (compensatory equalization), when subjects assigned to less-desirable treatments try to show that they can do just as well as those in treatment groups (compensatory rivalry), or when subjects in no-treatment control groups become demoralized and do less well than they otherwise would have (resentful demoralization).

Of course, one might take issue with any one of these problems. For example, it seems likely that one of Chen and Rossi's (1987) conditions—that there be no interactions between extraneous variables and treatment—is less a problem for molar causal inference than it is for the construct validity of treatment. And their first three conditions are less a problem for the logic of randomization than they are for the interpretation of individual experiments in which one or more conditions are not met. Nevertheless, all these points are well taken, at least in some respects. In fact, these problems seem all the more formidable because they are frequent in field research, such as AIDS research, where we often encounter small samples, heterogeneous samples, unreplicated experiments, nonrandom or differential attrition, important interactions, subjects who communicate with one another, administrators or caregivers who will not stand by and see clients assigned to treatments they think will not work, and patients who react emotionally and behaviorally about the treatment or control condition to which they have been assigned.

These are not just hypothetical problems. On the contrary, they are often encountered in field research. For example, in AIDS research, Valdisseri and others (1987) found that homosexual and bisexual men who agreed to participate in an AIDS education session were more likely to have had a college education than those who did not respond. Since better-educated people also tend to have more accurate knowledge about virtually all aspects of AIDS (National Center for Health Statistics, 1988), the study effectively sampled subjects who needed the intervention least and who probably represented only a minority of the population at risk. Similarly, AIDS researchers assume that infected patients who are assigned to treatment conditions will actively seek treatment from other sources, thus compromising the integrity of clinical trials. The implication is that, even if random procedures are often theoretically superior to other methods, they will encounter problems that have no easy solution and that thus make them biased in ways that we often cannot adjust for. Of course, we can always choose to ignore the presence of unknown but plausibly systematic biases on the grounds that this is the best we can do given current technology. But those grounds are defensible only to the extent that the researcher has just one possible method. However, the only thing that limits us to a single method in research is habit, disciplinary training, or simple narrow-mindedness.

The criticisms of random procedures just outlined are not the important ones, for they really argue only that we should complement our use of random procedures with some other procedures that might be able to compensate for their weaknesses. Random procedures still occupy center stage in such a scenario. But they begin to move to the side when we consider more serious objections that question the ability of random sampling or random assignment to bear some of the burdens that we encounter in field research. Two objections seem particularly important. First, even knowledgeable proponents of random sampling and random assignment recognize that they were not designed to address certain important research problems. Returning to the distinction between strategy and methods, we see that both random sampling and random assignment are matters of research method, not of research strategy. Since methods should always be subservient to strategy, it follows that the researcher must first and foremost be concerned with such strategic matters as the kind of question to be asked; the way in which the research project is to be implemented; how the data are to be analyzed; and how the results are to be interpreted and synthesized with the results of other studies that can shed some light on the same question. Neither random sampling nor random assignment have much to do with most of these strategic matters, but critical multiplism does.

When such procedures as randomization are placed in this context, it is easier to see how truly exceptional they are. They are exceptional both in the sense that they are unusually useful and accurate when we can apply them successfully and in the sense that they are the exception rather than the rule. That is, for most matters of research strategy, we do not have methods uniformly acknowledged to be superior even in principle. This is especially true for such matters as the generation of research questions or the interpretation of results, where we have very little understanding of how scientists generate options and choose among them. It is almost as true for the synthesis of research over multiple studies, where, for example, the fledgling methods of quantitative literature reviews are still the center of great controversy. It is even somewhat true for data analysis, for there are often several interesting and valid ways of analyzing the same data that yield different perspectives on it, a point that Coombs (1964) highlighted in his seminal work on measurement theory, *A Theory of Data.* In all these strategic matters, no single method is least biased. As a result, we should consider and implement multiple options, each having different biases.

The second serious objection to random procedures is that they are often not feasible in field settings. For example, consider random assignment to conditions. To be sure, such procedures are often far more feasible than they are said to be (Boruch, 1975; Boruch, McSweeny, and Soderstrom, 1978). We can even grant that such procedures may be significantly underutilized in field research and still be correct in asserting that there will be many important situations in which they are not feasible for reasons of logic, time, resources, skills, or logistics. Under these circumstances, there most often is no single best fallback position for facilitating causal inference and no single tactic that yields a least-biased answer. As a result, the best research strategy is to implement multiple options that do not share a single bias. For example, when randomized experiments are not feasible—and excepting these rare instances in which some of the strong quasi-experimental alternatives like time series or regression discontinuity can be used—there is often no single best tactic that yields a least-biased estimate of cause-and-effect relationships. The two major options—the various kinds of causal modeling and the use of quasi-experimental design features—both fail in different ways to deal with the problem adequately. Quasi-experimental design features are aimed at identifying the presence of threats to the validity of a causal inference, but they often can provide only limited estimates of the magnitude of causal effects, and they usually cannot eliminate the effects of many biases that they find to be present. Causal modeling techniques tend to rely on analysis of correlational data to adjust away bias and estimate the magnitude of effects, but their assumptions about our ability to know such biases completely and measure them perfectly are questionable. When, despite the different strengths and weaknesses of these techniques, the joint use of causal modeling and quasi-experimentation yields a convergent answer, our confidence in the causal inference is increased. It is even better if we implement each of these options in a multiplist mode, testing multiple causal models that vary in their assumptions about selection biases or the predictors of outcome and including in our models multiple quasi-experimental design features (multiple pretests, nonequivalent dependent variables, cohort controls), each selected to shed some light on a plausible bias (Shadish, Cook, and Houts, 1986).

Similar arguments apply to the feasibility and appropriateness of random sampling. Such sampling is most often successful when we sample from populations of persons or similar units, such as classrooms or hospital wards, for purposes of generalizing back to those populations. Yet there are many important research situations in which this is either not feasible or inappropriate to the generalization being sought. The most obvious situations are those in which the population at issue is not easily identified. The population of persons with AIDS or of persons susceptible to AIDS is an excellent example. In such situations, it may be more feasible to use alternatives to formal sampling from populations, such as sampling of presumed heterogeneous instances and of presumed modal instances (Cook and Campbell, 1979). Of course, we could always use a national random sample survey to estimate the magnitude of this population, but it would be certain from the outset that this survey would encounter important biasing feasibility problems (Turner, Fay, and Widdus, 1988). For example, if we used a household-based sampling frame, we would overlook some important groups, such as intravenous drug users, who are not attached to households but who are particularly susceptible to infection. No matter what the national sampling frame, some degree of nonresponse correlated with seropositivity is likely to occur, making estimates of this already low base rate characteristic all the more biased. A national random sampling study cannot solve all these problems. One excellent suggestion for dealing with this problem is to sample from respondents to a recent national survey, such as the Health Interview Survey, so that data from its interviews can be tapped in analyses of the biases that nonresponse may have caused (Turner, Fay, and Widdus, 1988). This is critical multiplism at its best, using multiple tactics that plausibly help to estimate and compensate for the biases in various sources.

Less obvious threats to the superiority of random sampling are the many situations in which we want to generalize but use a variety of tactics that have little or nothing to do with random sampling. In test construction, for example, modern formulations of classical test theory—domain sampling theory (Lord and Novick, 1968; Nunnally, 1978) or its extension in generalizability theory (Cronbach, Gleser, Nanda, and Rajaratnam, 1972)—allude to a sampling of items that in fact never takes place. Rather, generalization from the items to the construct of interest is justified on the basis of such tactics as the matching of item content with an explicated theory of the construct and on the basis of statistical covariations among items that make it plausible to think that they measure the same thing.

In still other situations, the notion of sampling to achieve generalization seems to disappear entirely. Consider, for example, the notion of generalization of causal connections (Cook, 1990). Cronbach (1982) approaches this task by seeking detailed explanations of the mediating links and mechanisms among inputs, causal processes, and outcomes, each of which is specified at a level of detail sufficient to clarify the essential mechanisms in each that are necessary to achieve the effect. According to this notion, generalization is facilitated by the fact that this detailed knowledge of mechanisms allows us to identify the essential elements, which we can transfer to new sites with increased confidence that the effect will be reproduced. Cronbach, in short, seeks generalization through theory, not sampling. Another approach, best represented by meta-analysis, seeks causal generalization through identification of robust causal connections that occur over a heterogeneous array of persons, settings, times, and cause-and-effect constructs. Such generalization is supported by two rationales. One rationale is induction—an effect observed over heterogeneous instances is more likely to appear in future instances not represented by any study in the current meta-analysis. The other rationale is falsification—the scientist deliberately seeks to find exceptions to the causal connection by varying instances within the existing data set. In meta-analysis, neither of these rationales relies explicitly on sampling or on Cronbach's notion of theory. If we examine all these instances of causal generalization in detail, we discover a multiplicity of tactics, each of which has advantages and disadvantages varying with the situation and none of which can uniformly be preferred to others over the many kinds of situations that scientists face (Cook, 1990).

In summary, then, it is probably wrong to object to critical multiplism on grounds that such procedures as random assignment and random sampling are uniformly superior. Not only is it wrong, it is also unfortunate, because such an objection suggests that random procedures somehow conflict with critical multiplism. Nothing could be further from the truth. Not only are random procedures in keeping with the best multiplist assumptions about making bias heterogeneous, but such procedures are no more than a small, special, tactical case of the general strategic approach represented by critical multiplism. Confusing tactics with strategy only clouds the issues involved.

The Reflexivity Problem. Does critical multiplism apply to itself? Yes. To be true to the themes of this chapter, therefore, there is one sense in which I must discourage widespread adoption of critical multiplism. After all, because no approach to inquiry is perfect, multiplism dictates that we encourage multiple approaches to be tried and then criticized. Indeed, such proliferation will inevitably continue as advocates of other positions develop them to their fullest and show what they can do that critical multiplism cannot do. The community of interested scholars will compare and contrast the strengths and weaknesses of each approach to find its biases of omission and commission. Eventually, our sense of the benefits of each approach will improve.

Of course, this very process is critically multiplist. That is one of the beauties of critical multiplism. Its advice applies perfectly well to itself. Those who follow the larger literature on science studies may recognize how hard it is to achieve such reflexivity without self-contradiction. For example, a key tenet of some social constructivist positions, especially the more radically deconstructionist ones, is that all knowledge is merely social construction and that no particular piece of knowledge is more valid than another. When applied reflexively, of course, this means that the approach called social constructivism is itself just a construction, hence no more valid than any other approach. At best, such a conclusion somewhat moderates the force of the position as a whole. At worst, it refutes it entirely. Discussions of this point among social constructivists never resolve the problem. Essentially, they argue that the benefits of deconstruction outweigh any problems caused by self-contradiction (Ashmore, 1989; Woolgar, 1988). Critical multiplism gives us the benefits without the contradiction. It encourages deconstruction, even of itself, without endorsing the nihilist extremes. It accepts the lack of firm foundations for knowledge without rejecting the possibility that some constructions of knowledge are better than others. Of course, the last point raises problems about how one distinguishes better from worse constructions, a point to which I now turn.

Does Critical Multiplism Mean Anything Goes? Another kind of objection is that critical multiplism flirts with a total rejection of standards for what is to count as a better or worse approach to the doing of science. Put as a simple question, can critical multiplism be distinguished from philosopher Paul Feyerabend's (1975, p. 28) speculation about whether "anything goes"? This criticism is particularly astute because the notion that anything goes is similar to critical multiplism in some less than obvious epistemological ways. In particular, while it is always difficult to trace the influences of other people's work on the development of an idea, it is probably accurate to suggest that one intellectual root of multiplism is Campbell's (1974) notion of blind variations in evolutionary epistemology. He draws an analogy between the way in which species evolve biologically and the way in which knowledge develops in science and other areas. Central to both kinds of evolution is the availability of radically different alternatives that help to cope with a problem in a truly new and perhaps more effective way. The argument is that an alternative is less likely to cope with a problem differently precisely in the degree to which it resembles what already exists. Hence, truly novel variations are needed. In biological evolution, these variations are accomplished by means of random genetic mutation. By analogy, evolutionary epistemology requires a similar mechanism. The analogy begins to break down at this point, because we cannot say what mechanism serves this random permutations function in science. But some version of multiplism is a likely candidate.

One feature distinguishes this multiplism from anything goes: criticism. Multiplism encourages us to explore diverse options. But such exploration is not an end in itself. Rather, each option must be evaluated for its ability to solve problems in the relevant research. In essence, we must ask four questions of each option: First, will a bias of omission or commission be incurred if we do not implement the option? Second, will the option reduce that bias better than other options now available, or will it at least reduce bias below current levels? Third, can we estimate the direction and magnitude of these biases for the option? Fourth, if multiple biases are associated with the option, can we combine our assessments of their direction and magnitude in a way that enables us to make an overall judgment about the value of the option?

In operationalizing this logic, we must keep in mind that, although many biases are possible, not all are plausible. In critical multiplism, plausible biases always take priority over possible biases that are not obviously plausible. This corollary is necessary in order to avoid an infinite regress that allows anything goes to return because we cannot exclude any possible bias, no matter how implausible it may be. Thus, any operationalization of these four questions is plausible precisely to the degree that it is not inconsistent with such criteria as reason, experience, or observation. How plausible a bias is determines the priority that we must assign to its study. Ultimately, of course, these judgments of plausibility are as fallible as other kinds of human knowledge, and so they will be subject to revision and reinterpretation over time (Lakatos, 1978). We may thus have to conceptualize plausibility in Bayesian terms, constantly adjusting our estimated plausibilities in light of new evidence. Sometimes we may not know exactly in which direction to make these adjustments, especially if there are several plausible biases, each of which may operate in different directions to produce either a positive or a negative effect (Mark and Shotland, 1985). Even when the scientist has absolutely no indication which bias is more plausible, he or she is better off for having taken the critical multiplist approach because identifying plausible biases points to questions for future research.

Valid Objections to Critical Multiplism

Certain problems need further attention before critical multiplism can be as practical as required. The pages that follow describe some of these difficulties and the directions that possible remedies might take.

What Is Bias? The term *bias* figures prominently in the present discussion. Yet I have deliberately left it ambiguous, primarily because what counts as a bias varies with the different tasks that scientists must perform. Statistics is the context in which the notion of bias is clearest: Bias implies some systematic (that is, nonrandom) distortion so that the value of a statistic is no longer "true." Statisticians speak of *biased* estimators, *biased* samples, and *biased* tests. They can also speak of, say, linear *unbiased* estimators and asymptotically *unbiased* estimators. In this sense, too, we may say that random samples yield asymptotically *unbiased* estimates of their population parameters or that randomized experiments with no attrition yield *unbiased* estimates of treatment effects. In these last expressions, *bias* has a highly stylized and formal meaning.

Unfortunately, most scientific tasks are not as clear-cut as statistics, so the meaning of *bias* changes accordingly. However, in most uses it retains the notion that some systematic phenomenon interferes with the inferences that we want to make, but it loses the notion that some "true" value is being distorted. For example, if we say that a certain researcher is biased against a certain theory, we mean that his or her visible behaviors favor one theory over another, even if we do not know which theory is true—or even whether a theory is true. Similarly, if we say that some literature is biased by its failure to examine a certain perspective, we do not need to know whether that perspective is true in order to note that the literature is biased.

In general, then, bias is an error of omission or commission that leaves us either with knowledge that is in some plausible respect wrong or misleading or without certain kinds of knowledge that are plausibly needed. For example, the general failure in AIDS research to ask questions about women and AIDS may leave us without information that we may need to cope with future extensions of the AIDS epidemic into the heterosexual community. Our failure to ask about the socioeconomic causes of AIDS among prostitutes may deprive us of a significant option for treating the disease in that population. Our failure to use ipsative measurement strategies like rank ordering and paired comparison techniques in research design may cost us accurate knowledge about the general public's perceptions of the relative risks in the various ways in which AIDS can be transmitted. These are all plausible biases of omission or commission.

Bias is also particularistic and fallible. It is particularistic in the sense that the arguments both for and against it necessarily have to appeal to particular, specialized knowledge that is germane to the research topic at hand. For example, in justifying why one thinks that randomized experiments are more conducive to causal inference than other methods, we must appeal to concepts and methods involving the nature of causation, the nature of statistical probability, and our inability to specify selection biases with the degree of precision that we would like. But our arguments will also be fallible, because they are based on assumptions about such things as causation, probability theory, and the magnitude of selection biases that may be incorrect in some way; because they require method to be implemented with a theoretical fidelity that practice often belies; and because they are always subject to revision as new observations and theories render them obsolete. Therefore, exploration of the nature of bias preferentially occurs at the particularistic, not the general, level. I have provided some examples of how we can make such applications in the context of past work on quasi-experimentation (Shadish, Cook, and Houts, 1986), long-term care for the chronically mentally ill (Shadish, 1986), and the person-situation debate (Houts, Cook, and Shadish, 1986).

Thus, what we need are ways to explore, define, and estimate such biases across a variety of domains. At least four directions seem promising in this regard. The first is Monte Carlo modeling. For example, Zwick and Velicer (1986) describe five different ways of determining the number of factors to extract from a correlation matrix during a factor analysis. They found that the eigenvalue-greater-than-one rule systematically tends to extract too many factors from a matrix. While Monte Carlo methods have most often been applied to statistical problems, it seems that we could easily use them to examine a wider array of methodological and design problems.

A second way of estimating biases is by adapting meta-analysis to the task (Glass, McGaw, and Smith, 1981; Hedges and Olkin, 1985). Meta-analysis has mostly been used to review studies for the substantive conclusions that they yield about a topic, as in the numerous meta-analyses of whether psychotherapy works (Smith, Glass, and Miller, 1980). But a growing number of scientists are interested in the use of meta-analysis to examine the effects of tactics and methodologies on the results of research. Most prominent have been the many examinations of whether randomized experiments and quasi-experiments yield different effects (Smith, Glass, and Miller, 1980). Another example is empirical studies of the biases in published studies relative to so-called file-drawer (that is, unpublished) studies (Shadish, Doherty, and Montgomery, 1989). Meta-analysis seems to have enormous potential for improving our empirical understanding of the tactical biases in research.

The third way of estimating bias is to manipulate particular tactical options experimentally to see whether they produce different results. Much of this kind of work has been done in survey research. For example, Bradburn and others (1979) were interested in investigating biases that might result from the various ways in which threatening questions could be asked. They randomly assigned respondents to one of four conditions: personal interview, telephone survey, self-administered questionnaire, or the random response method. They found both that "no one method is clearly superior to all others" and that "the random response method does appear to produce less underreporting for very threatening questions" (Bradburn and others, 1979, p. 167).

The fourth way is through better observation, description, and measurement of the methodological features of research about which we currently know very little. Examples include Haveman's (1985) description of the costs and benefits of social experiments; LaLonde's (1986) description of empirical differences between randomized experiments and selection bias modeling in estimations of the effects of social interventions; and Latour and Woolgar's (1979) description of the ways in which laboratory scientists form questions, shape data, and interpret results. Especially in this last area—we know so little about how scientists proceed—discovery-oriented methods may be most appropriate for our first attempts at exploring the biases that may be at work.

While the volume of research on bias seems to be increasing rapidly, there is still far too little of it, and it tends to be scattered across literatures and mostly to be limited to traditional statistical and methodological matters. If we are to have a truly practical critical multiplism, we must have more such studies, their implications for the conduct of research have to be better integrated, and—perhaps most important—they need to be extended to such relatively overlooked but critical tactical matters as formation of questions, interpretation of results, integration of findings over multiple studies, and dissemination and use of scientific knowledge.

Biases That Everyone Shares. Another problem with critical multiplism is that when all available theories or methods share the same bias, even multiplistic criticism may be incapable of revealing it. This criticism is a version of the notion shared by contemporary philosophers of science that we can never really know that we have uncovered the "truth" (Lakatos, 1978; Laudan, 1977). While this is a serious problem, it does not mean that critical multiplism is less worthy than other strategies for the conduct of science, because shared biases have proved to be a major stumbling block in all science. In fact, I know of no technique for ensuring that all such bias has been avoided, so I will grant that all knowledge is presumptive rather than "true." I would only hypothesize that critical multiplism is more likely than other strategies to uncover these shared biases when they exist.

Social Psychological Resistance. One important problem with critical multiplism is that efforts to implement it are likely to meet social and psychological resistance from scientists. Recall that the need for the social psychological component of critical multiplism arose from scientists' inability to identify the biases in their own work. Some of these limitations are psychological. For example, even with the best intentions, human beings are finite in their capacity to see all the alternative questions, designs, analyses, and interpretations that could characterize a study (Faust, 1984). Failing to see those alternatives, they tend to reach premature closure that an issue is settled. Another psychological limitation involves the biases that seem to be a part of human nature. That is, all scientists are human beings who seem to be subject to many of the same psychological and social biases that we can observe among other human beings (Faust, 1984; Mahoney, 1976). Like all humans, scientists are prone to ignore whether their predictions exceed base rates, to draw unwarranted generalizations from a small number of observations, to misinterpret regression artifacts as real causal agency, and to pay attention to things that confirm their favorite theories while passing over things that refute them (Faust, 1984). Both scientists (Mahoney, 1976; Mitroff and Fitzgerald, 1977) and nonscientists (Bradley, 1981) tend to be passionately committed to their favorite hypotheses and express great confidence in their opinions even in the face of contradictory evidence or simply when guessing about an ambiguous matter.

Other factors that prevent scientists from recognizing the biases in their work are sociological and social psychological in character. For example, Lacy and Busch (1983) found that scientists reported communicating with colleagues outside their departments less than once a month, although they also reported that contacts with such colleagues were a major source of their research ideas. As a result, the authors point out, their communication takes on an "insular" pattern. Similarly, Mahoney (1985) notes that disciplinary structures, peer review processes, and tenure proceedings all tend to discourage the free exchange of novel and critical ideas essential to epistemic progress. Descriptions of how these matters can lead to problems in science abound. For examples, I point to Franks's (1981) description of the polywater episode and to Watson's (1968) description of DNA research.

The net effect of these social and psychological factors is that scientists are probably not sufficiently skeptical of their own work and that they probably do not receive sufficient criticism from diverse sources. Each factor is a two-edged sword! Both are reasons why scientists need criticism, and both are reasons why we can expect that scientists will resist criticism. If scientists are often too finite to recognize the multiple biases associated with their own work, if they too rarely seek and use serious criticism to help uncover those biases, and if disciplinary and other sociological structures often protect them from criticism, how can we be optimistic that critical multiplism will be adopted unless these factors are changed? Introducing science to critical multiplism may require changing the sociology and psychology of science. But we know that wholesale changes in social structures and personal beliefs and behaviors do not occur quickly or easily (Lindblom, 1977; Lindblom and Cohen, 1979; Shadish, 1984). This is probably as true of scientific change as it is of any other form of social change (Neimeyer and Shadish, 1987).

Adopting Critical Multiplism at the Individual Level. Felix Franks (1981) suggested that the pathologies in science that gave rise to the polywater controversy are at least partly a function of the way in which individual scientists think about their work. As he noted, "Michael Faraday once expressed the hope that fifty years after his death nothing he had ever written would still be considered true. Most scientists of today lack Faraday's modesty; they like to believe that everything they commit to paper will endure as truth forever. Genuine changes of heart or mind are therefore suspect" (Franks, 1981, p. 190).

Getting individual scientists to change this mind-set and adopt a critical multiplist perspective on their work may require instilling this attitude during initial training. Many scientific habits and ways of thinking are probably set during that time, and they may be more difficult to change later in a scientific career. If I were to design a course on research design for graduate students in psychology, for example, a reading outlining the tenets of critical multiplism and showing how it can be applied would figure prominently, although whether this reading should occur early or later in the course could be debated. Moreover, such courses often ask students to criticize the methodology of published studies. It should prove easy to add a critical multiplist component to such exercises first by selecting multiple studies that illustrate the topic being discussed, then by having students suggest new ways of doing the study and criticize any constant biases they found in the ones already done. Critical multiplism could also figure prominently in any courses discussing cognate ideas from the philosophy of science, such as logical positivism—assuming, of course, that novice scientists still take such courses.

Nevertheless, there are likely to be fundamental limits on the degree to which individual scientists can be critically multiplistic, if for no other reason than human finitude. For example, it is unrealistic to expect any single scientist to know how to conduct every possible statistical technique that might be relevant, from survival analysis to linear structural modeling via logistic regression. It is only slightly more realistic to hope that, with diligent effort that will probably have to extend well beyond graduate training, scientists can learn to recognize that there are relevant alternative options and that it might be appropriate to seek help in implementing them—so that they at least will know what survival analysis is, what it does, and when it can be relevant to their work, even if they cannot conduct such analysis themselves. Ultimately, individual scientists must fail even at this latter task, which is why the social component of critical multiplism is essential and also why it is wrong to think of critical multiplism as a state of mind of the individual scientist without a necessary social component.

In much the same way, even if one agrees in principle with the idea that scientists should be skeptical critics of their own and others' work, the demands of scientific practice can militate against the principle. Practice prefers the simple, the black-and-white, the easily implementable and codifiable course of action. A constant search for complexity could easily paralyze practice. Hence, there will inevitably be tension between critical multiplism and the demands of practice that the corollary technical guidelines outlined earlier can only partly remedy.

Finally, there may also be limitations on the degree to which scientists should be critically multiplistic, at least for some scientists performing some tasks in some stages of research. Mitroff's study of the Apollo moon scientists (Mitroff and Fitzgerald, 1977) gives most pause for concern here.

Mitroff found that the scientists whom their peers regarded as the most creative, influential, and visionary were the scientists who most stubbornly pursued their single favorite theory, even in the face of potentially serious conflicting evidence. Such pursuit is somewhat antithetical to critical multiplism, yet it is nonetheless justified both to test the limits of a theory (Lakatos, 1978) and to allow for the modicum of personal passion that is probably one essential ingredient of good science. As Popper (1972, p. 12) put it, "critical reasoning is better than passion, especially in matters touching on logic. But I am quite ready to admit that nothing will ever be achieved without a modicum of passion." Thus, some scientists may work best without being very self-critical. Yet, having successfully (and passionately) applied critical multiplism myself to the analysis of several theoretical and methodological problems (Houts, Cook, and Shadish, 1986; Shadish, Cook, and Houts, 1986), I am reluctant to endorse Mitroff's description of science as uniformly best for all good scientists. At a minimum, then, we need much more research on the social psychology of science if we are to understand when and why both passion and criticism should enter the research process (Gholson, Shadish, Neimeyer, and Houts, 1989; Shadish and Fuller, in press). I am therefore much more tentative about advocating critical multiplism at the individual level than I am at the social and institutional level.

Adopting Critical Multiplism at the Institutional Level. It seems more likely that the successful introduction of critical multiplism into science will have to come at the institutional and social level. This has long been Don Campbell's argument, and his recent work on the sociology of scientific validity bears witness to his continued creativity in suggesting practical ways in which science can be both critical and multiple. Perhaps the best example is his article on monitoring the scientific competence of the National Institute of Mental Health's (NIMH) Preventive Intervention Research Centers (Campbell, 1987). He makes a number of suggestions for improving scientific competence in these centers: Fund annual conferences on prevention research that would enable center staff to share current progress. Encourage problem overlap in research both within and between centers, and foster diversity of method among individual approaches to the same problem. Allow several scientists in the same center to submit independent grant applications. Split large studies into two or more parallel studies. Fund cross-validation research for the implementation of promising prevention interventions. Facilitate reanalysis and meta-analysis. Encourage grant final reports to include an appendix indicating how the investigator would redesign the study if he or she could do it over again. Legitimate and facilitate supplementary and dissenting-opinion research reports from research staff in forms ranging from simple dissenting footnotes to secondary analysis and publication by dissenting authors of alternative findings and interpretations. Finally, give preference for funding to authors with established interdisciplinary publication records over those with narrower disciplinary focuses. Of course, not all these suggestions will prove effective or practical (Neimeyer and Shadish, 1987). But on the whole, too few theorists—including me—are thinking of ways that might make critical multiplism more widely used in science. That is one of the tasks on my own list of future articles. Undoubtedly, I will borrow heavily from the work of sociologists of science and from science policy analysts (Averch, 1985; Latour, 1987) in this kind of elaboration.

Practical Problems. Even if one were to accept all these points in principle, a few practical problems would make the use of critical multiplism difficult even for the truest of true believers. One is that a manuscript or a grant application developed in a critical multiplist mode is not likely to be well received. Critical multiplism is a tool for generating and criticizing options before you begin writing about those ideas. But once you have finished developing the ideas and you begin writing, the practical task is different—to weave as compelling a story as you can about the ideas on which you eventually settled. At that point, a complete list of the rejected options is distracting. One should no more lead the reader through the process that generated the good ideas than one should lead the reader through all the steps of every statistical analysis that one does of the data. In grant proposals and journal articles, we mostly show readers the results of our work, not the processes that we went through in getting to those results. It might be better if this were not so, but this is probably a fact of scientific writing.

Another worry raised by critical multiplism is that political or social reasons will make some novel options not very acceptable to colleagues, funding agencies, or society. For instance, one administrator in the National Institutes of Health told me that he would love to have grant proposals that looked at problems in truly novel ways but that, in his experience, review panels, especially those dominated by one discipline or specialty, tended to reject proposals for research that obviously departed from accepted paradigms. This is a good point. It takes a good deal of seasoned judgment and experience to know just exactly how novel one can afford to be and still get funded or published. Similarly, it is risky to submit a proposal that questions fundamental assumptions about the way in which things get done or that conflicts in important ways with the political and economic structures within which one works. The reason is not just the political risks incumbent in such proposals but also that the truly radical proposals would be extremely difficult to implement in public policy, no matter how effective they might prove to be. Inevitably, some of the options generated by a critical multiplist approach will be of this type, and they should be proposed only with great hesitation—particularly by younger, untenured, or otherwise insecure researchers. The best advice here is to get input from an experienced scholar before submitting such a proposal—not just any scholar but one who has experience with review panels or publication outlets like the one to which you plan to submit..

Having said this, it is incumbent on me to note that many of the options generated through critical multiplism will not be antiestablishment. Rather, they will simply identify gaps in our knowledge that the granting agencies themselves may welcome having filled. For example, a colleague of mine has long been interested in research to prevent smoking. He started by trying interventions to help people quit. But there was always a hard core of smokers who would not quit or who soon relapsed if they did quit. On exploring their reasons, he discovered that they often complained that they gained weight after they quit, and research verified the complaint. He explored differences between males and females and found both that the weight gain was much more pronounced in females and that females had rarely been studied in smoking research. Hence, he proposed an array of projects exploring this problem in females. Was it antiestablishment? Quite the contrary. Agencies like the NIH have recognized the weaknesses of the monism in so much of our biomedical and health services research under which even the rats are white males. Such agencies were quite anxious to receive proposals on other populations. As these examples suggest, taking a critical multiplist stance often helps generate ideas that are neither antiestablishment or antiparadigm but rather that point to important gaps in our knowledge that many people want to see filled.

Finally, it is not possible to be fully critically multiplist in any given study. Time, resource, and skill constraints simply make it impossible to follow all options at once. Nor is it necessarily desirable to be fully critical multiplist in a series of closely related studies on a given problem. After all, one could not replicate a finding or fine-tune one's understanding of the results of a study if one changed the original conceptualization, design, execution, or analysis in any radical way. Rather, critical multiplism is probably a goal better suited for certain tasks and levels of effort than others: for programs of research rather than single studies; for the "invisible colleges" of researchers working competitively and cooperatively on the same problem whose members carve out a niche for themselves by identifying the gaps and problems in the relevant literature; for reconceptualizing an area in which progress has reached a standstill; for making sure that one's research is not getting into a conceptual or methodological rut; for generating important variations within one's program of research that are likely to make a real difference to the outcome; and, within single studies, for increasing the odds that one has not overlooked an important version of a question, an important measure, an important analysis, an important objection to what one has done, or any other of the reasonably inexpensive options that we could include in our studies with very little extra cost or effort.

Perhaps the point to remember in all this is the value of criticism, whether it be critical multiplism in one's program of research or critical monism in a single study. In all cases, it is always better to know one's strengths and weaknesses. But it is easier to be multiplist than it is to be critical. Good criticism is a precious commodity, difficult to find the energy to do and difficult to hear from others. Good criticism does not just come up with alternatives but with alternatives that make an important difference for the results.

Conclusion

A colleague prominently displays the following quotation on his office door:

> When someone is honestly 55 percent right, that's very good and there's no use wrangling. And if someone is 60 percent right, it's wonderful, it's great luck, and let him thank God. But what's to be said about 75 percent right? Wise people say this is suspicious. Well, and what about 100 percent right? Whoever says he's 100 percent right is a fanatic, a thug, and the worst kind of rascal.

The old Jew of Galicia to whom this remark is attributed has captured the kind of skepticism advocated in critical multiplism. Probably no scientist and no scientific study are ever 100 percent right. We can only hope that, if we do our job properly and with sufficient critical perspective, we may be slightly more often right than wrong—55 percent right, so to speak. But we should always keep in mind how close we are to being more often wrong than right—even a slip to 45 percent right would mean that we would be mostly wrong. In social science, we often work in this small margin. We need every tool at our disposal to help us to produce results that in the long run fall on the right side of the distribution.

References

Ashmore, M. *The Reflexive Thesis: Wrighting the Sociology of Scientific Knowledge*. Chicago: University of Chicago Press, 1989.

Averch, H. A. *A Strategic Analysis of Science and Technology Policy*. Baltimore, Md.: Johns Hopkins University Press, 1985.

Bechtel, W. *Philosophy of Science: An Overview for Cognitive Science*. Hillsdale, N.J.: Erlbaum, 1988.

Bem, D. J. "Constructing a Theory of the Triple Typology: Some (Second) Thoughts on Nomothetic and Idiographic Approaches to Personality." *Journal of Personality*, 1983, *51*, 566–577.

Bem, D. J., and Allen, A. "On Predicting Some of the People Some of the Time: The Search for Cross-Situational Consistencies in Behavior." *Psychological Review*, 1974, *81*, 506–520.

Boruch, R. F. "On Common Contentions About Randomized Field Experiments." In R. F. Boruch and H. W. Reicken (eds.), *Experimental Testing of Public Policy: The Proceedings of the 1974 Social Science Research Council Conference on Social Experiments.* Boulder, Colo.: Westview Press, 1975.

Boruch, R. F., McSweeny, A. J., and Soderstrom, E. J. "Randomized Field Experiments for Program Planning, Development, and Evaluation: An Illustrative Bibliography." *Evaluation Quarterly,* 1978, *2,* 655–695.

Bradburn, N. M., Sudman, S., Blair, E., Locander, W., Miles, C., Singer, E., and Stocking, C. *Improving Interview Methods and Questionnaire Design.* San Francisco: Jossey-Bass, 1979.

Bradley, J. V. "Overconfidence in Ignorant Experts." *Bulletin of the Psychonomic Society,* 1981, *17,* 82–84.

Buss, D. M., and Craik, K. H. "The Act Frequency Approach to Personality." *Psychological Review,* 1983, *90,* 105–126.

Buss, D. M., and Craik, K. H. "Acts, Dispositions, and Personality." In B. A. Maher and W. B. Maher (eds.), *Progress in Experimental Personality Research.* Vol. 13. New York: Academic Press, 1984.

Campbell, D. T. "Evolutionary Epistemology." In P. A. Schilpp (ed.), *The Philosophy of Karl Popper.* La Salle, Ill.: Open Court, 1974.

Campbell, D. T. "Guidelines for Monitoring the Scientific Competence of Preventive Intervention Research Centers: An Exercise in the Sociology of Scientific Validity." *Knowledge: Creation, Diffusion, Utilization,* 1987, 8, 389–430.

Campbell, D. T., and Fiske, D. W. "Convergent and Discriminant Validity by the Multitrait-Multimethod Matrix." *Psychological Bulletin,* 1959, *56,* 81–105.

Campbell, D. T., and Stanley, J. C. *Experimental and Quasi-experimental Designs for Research.* Skokie, Ill.: Rand McNally, 1963.

Chen, H., and Rossi, P. H. "The Theory-Driven Approach to Validity." *Evaluation and Program Planning,* 1987, *10,* 95–103.

Cicirelli, V. G., and Associates. *The Impact of Head Start: An Evaluation of the Effects of Head Start on Children's Cognitive and Affective Development. A Report to the Office of Economic Opportunity.* Athens: Ohio University and Westinghouse Learning Corporation, 1969.

Cook, T. D. "Postpositivist Critical Multiplism." In L. Shotland and M. M. Mark (eds.), *Social Science and Social Policy.* Newbury Park, Calif.: Sage, 1985.

Cook, T. D. "The Generalization of Causal Connections: Theories in Search of Clear Practice." In L. Sechrest, E. Perrin, and J. Bunker (eds.), *Research Methodology: Strengthening Causal Interpretations of Nonexperimental Data.* Publication No. (PHS) 90-3435. Rockville, Md.: National Center for Health Services Research and Health Care Technology Assessment, Public Health Service, U.S. Department of Health and Human Services, 1990.

Cook, T. D., and Campbell, D. T. *Quasi-experimentation: Design and Analysis Issues for Field Settings.* Skokie, Ill.: Rand McNally, 1979.

Cook, T. D., and Reichardt, C. S. (eds.). *Qualitative and Quantitative Methods in Evaluation Research.* Newbury Park, Calif.: Sage, 1979.

Coombs, C. *A Theory of Data.* New York: Wiley, 1964.

Cronbach, L. J. *Designing Evaluations of Educational and Social Programs.* San Francisco: Jossey-Bass, 1982.

Cronbach, L. J., Gleser, G., Nanda, H., and Rajaratnam, N. *The Dependability of Behavioral Measurements: Theory of Generalizability for Scores and Profiles.* New York: Wiley, 1972.

Davies, P.C.W., and Brown, J. R. *The Ghost in the Atom.* Cambridge, England: Cambridge University Press, 1986.

Dawes, R. M. "Measurement Models for Rating and Comparing Risks: The Context of AIDS." In L. Sechrest, H. Freeman, and A. Mulley (eds.), *Health Services Research Methodology: A Focus on AIDS.* Publication No. (PHS) 89-3439. Rockville, Md.: National Center for Health Services Research and Health Care Technology Assessment, Public Health Service,

U.S. Department of Health and Human Services, 1989.

D'Espagnat, B. *In Search of Reality*. New York: Springer-Verlag, 1983.

Dunn, W. N. "Reforms as Arguments." *Knowledge: Creation, Diffusion, Utilization*, 1982, *3*, 293–326.

Epstein, S. "The Stability of Behavior: On Predicting Most of the People Much of the Time." *Journal of Personality and Social Psychology*, 1979, *37*, 1097–1126.

Faust, D. *The Limits of Scientific Reasoning*. Minneapolis: University of Minnesota Press, 1984.

Feyerabend, P. *Against Method: Outline of an Anarchistic Theory of Knowledge*. London: Verso, 1975.

Fisher, R. A. *Statistical Methods for Research Workers*. London: Oliver & Boyd, 1925.

Franks, F. *Polywater*. Cambridge, Mass.: MIT Press, 1981.

Garfield, E. "Is Citation Analysis a Legitimate Evaluation Tool?" *Scientometrics*, 1979, *1*, 359–375.

Gholson, B., and Barker, P. "Kuhn, Lakatos, and Laudan: Applications in the History of Physics and Psychology." *American Psychologist*, 1985, *40*, 755–769.

Gholson, B. G., Shadish, W. R., Neimeyer, R. A., and Houts, A. C. (eds.). *Psychology of Science: Contributions to Metascience*. Cambridge, England: Cambridge University Press, 1989.

Glass, G. V., McGaw, B., and Smith, M. L. *Meta-analysis in Social Research*. Newbury Park, Calif.: Sage, 1981.

Groopman, J. E., Salahuddin, S. Z., Sarngadharan, M. G., Markham, P. D., Gonda, M., Sliski, A., and Gallo, R. C. "HTLV-III in Saliva of People with AIDS-Related Complex and Healthy Homosexual Men at Risk for AIDS." *Science*, 1984, *226*, 447–449.

Haveman, R. H. "Social Experimentation and Social Experimentation." *Journal of Human Resources*, 1985, *21*, 586–605.

Hedges, L. V., and Olkin, I. *Statistical Methods for Meta-analysis*. Orlando, Fla.: Academic Press, 1985.

Ho, D. D., Byington, R. E., Schooley, R. T., Flynn, T., Rota, T. R., and Hirsch, M. S. "Infrequency of Isolation of HTLV-III Virus from Saliva in AIDS." *New England Journal of Medicine*, 1985, *313*, 1606.

Houts, A. C., Cook, T. D., and Shadish, W. R. "The Person-Situation Debate: A Critical Multiplist Perspective." *Journal of Personality*, 1986, *54*, 101–154.

Keller, E. F. *A Feeling for the Organism*. San Francisco: Freeman, 1983.

Kinsey, A. C., Pomeroy, W. B., and Martin, C. E. *Sexual Behavior in the Human Male*. Philadelphia: Saunders, 1948.

Kuhn, T. S. *The Structure of Scientific Revolutions*. (2nd ed.) Chicago: University of Chicago Press, 1970.

Lacy, W. B., and Busch, L. "Informal Scientific Communication in the Agricultural Sciences." *Information Processing and Management*, 1983, *19*, 193–202.

Lagakos, S. "Statistical Analysis of Survival Data, with Applications to the AIDS Epidemic." In L. Sechrest, H. Freeman, and A. Mulley (eds.), *Health Services Research Methodology: A Focus on AIDS*. Publication No. (PHS) 89-3439. Rockville, Md.: National Center for Health Services Research and Health Care Technology Assessment, Public Health Service, U.S. Department of Health and Human Services, 1989.

Lakatos, I. *The Methodology of Scientific Research Programmes: Philosophical Papers*. Vol. 1. Cambridge, England: Cambridge University Press, 1978.

LaLonde, R. J. "Evaluating the Econometric Evaluations of Training Programs with Experimental Data." *American Economic Review*, 1986, *76*, 604–620.

Latour, B. *Science in Action*. Cambridge, Mass.: Harvard University Press, 1987.

Latour, B., and Woolgar, S. *Laboratory Life: The Social Construction of Scientific Facts*. London: Sage, 1979.

Laudan, L. *Progress and Its Problems: Towards a Theory of Scientific Growth.* Berkeley: University of California Press, 1977.

Lewin, R. "A Naturalist of the Genome." *Science,* 1983, *222,* 402–405.

Lindblom, C. E. *Politics and Markets: The World's Political-Economic Systems.* New York: Basic Books, 1977.

Lindblom, C. E., and Cohen, D. K. *Usable Knowledge: Social Science and Social Problem Solving.* New Haven, Conn.: Yale University Press, 1979.

Lord, F. M., and Novick, M. R. *Statistical Theories of Mental Test Scores.* Reading, Mass.: Addison-Wesley, 1968.

Lowry, O. H., Rosenbrough, N. J., Farr, A. L., and Randall, R. J. "Protein Measurement with the Folin Phenol Reagent." *Journal of Biological Chemistry,* 1951, *193,* 265–275.

Magidson, J. "Toward a Causal-Model Approach for Adjusting for Preexisting Differences in the Nonequivalent Control Group Situation: A General Alternative to ANCOVA." *Evaluation Quarterly,* 1977, *1,* 399–420.

Mahoney, M. J. *Psychologist as Subject: The Psychological Imperative.* Cambridge, Mass.: Ballinger, 1976.

Mahoney, M. J. "Open Exchange and Epistemic Progress." *American Psychologist,* 1985, *40,* 29–39.

Mark, M. M., and Shotland, R. L. "Toward More Useful Social Science." In R. L. Shotland and M. M. Mark (eds.), *Social Science and Social Policy.* Newbury Park, Calif.: Sage, 1985.

Meehl, P. E. "What Social Scientists Don't Understand." In D. W. Fiske and R. A. Shweder (eds.), *Metatheory in Social Science.* Chicago: University of Chicago Press, 1986.

Mischel, W. "On the Interface of Cognition and Personality: Beyond the Person-Situation Debate." *American Psychologist,* 1979, *34,* 740–754.

Mischel, W., and Peake, P. K. "Beyond Deja Vu in Search for Cross-Situational Consistency." *Psychological Review,* 1982, *89,* 730–755.

Mitroff, I. I., and Fitzgerald, I. "On the Psychology of the Apollo Moon Scientists: A Chapter in the Psychology of Science." *Human Relations,* 1977, *130,* 657–674.

Naisbitt, J. *Megatrends: Ten New Directions Transforming Our Lives.* New York: Warner Books, 1984.

National Center for Health Statistics. "AIDS Knowledge and Attitudes for October 1987: Provisional Data from the National Health Interview Survey." In *Advance Data from Vital and Health Statistics,* no. 150. Publication No. (PHS) 88-1250. Hyattsville, Md.: Public Health Service, U.S. Department of Health and Human Services, 1988.

Neimeyer, R. A., and Shadish, W. R. "Optimizing Scientific Validity: Toward an Interdisciplinary Science Studies." *Knowledge: Creation, Diffusion, Utilization,* 1987, *8,* 463–485.

Nunnally, J. C. *Psychometric Theory.* (2nd ed.) New York: McGraw-Hill, 1978.

Popper, K. R. *Objective Knowledge: An Evolutionary Approach.* Oxford, England: Oxford University Press, 1972.

Rae, A. *Quantum Physics: Illusion or Reality?* Cambridge, England: Cambridge University Press, 1986.

Rein, M., and Schon, D. A. "Problem Setting in Policy Research." In C. H. Weiss (ed.), *Using Social Research in Public Policy-Making.* Lexington, Mass.: Lexington Books, 1977.

Rindskopf, D. M. "Structural Equation Models in Analysis of Nonexperimental Data." In R. F. Boruch, P. M. Wortman, and D. S. Cordray (eds.), *Reanalyzing Program Evaluations.* San Francisco: Jossey-Bass, 1981.

Rossi, P. H., Berk, R. A., and Lenihan, K. J. *Money, Work, and Crime: Some Experimental Evidence.* New York: Academic Press, 1980.

Rossi, P. H., Wright, J. D., and Anderson, A. (eds.). *Handbook of Survey Research.* New York: Academic Press, 1983.

Schreeder, M. T., Thompson, S. E., Hadler, S. C., Berquist, K. R., Zaidi, A., Maynard, J. E., Judson, N., Broff, E. H., Nylund, T., Moore, J. N., Gardner, P., Doto, I. L., and Reynolds,

G. "Hepatitis B in Homosexual Men: Prevalence of Infection and Factors Related to Transmission." *Journal of Infectious Diseases,* 1982, *146,* 7–15.

Shadish, W. R. "Policy Research: Lessons from the Implementation of Deinstitutionalization." *American Psychologist,* 1984, *39,* 725–738.

Shadish, W. R. "Planned Critical Multiplism: Some Elaborations." *Behavioral Assessment,* 1986, *8,* 75–103.

Shadish, W. R., Cook, T. D., and Houts, A. C. "Quasi-experimentation in a Critical Multiplist Mode." In W.M.K. Trochim (ed.), *Advances in Quasi-experimental Design and Analysis.* New Directions for Program Evaluation, no. 81. San Francisco: Jossey-Bass, 1986.

Shadish, W. R., Cook, T. D., and Leviton, L. C. *Foundations of Program Evaluation: Theories of Practice.* Newbury Park, Calif.: Sage, 1991.

Shadish, W. R., Doherty, M., and Montgomery, L. M. "How Many Studies Are in the File Drawer? An Estimate from the Family/Marital Psychotherapy Literature." *Clinical Psychology Review,* 1989, *9,* 589–603.

Shadish, W. R., and Fuller, S. (eds.). *Social Psychology of Science: The Psychological Turn.* New York: Guilford, in press.

Shadish, W. R., and Reis, J. "A Review of the Effectiveness of Programs to Improve Pregnancy Outcome." *Evaluation Review,* 1984, *8,* 747–776.

Sharpe, T. R., and Wetherbee, H. *Final Report: Evaluation of the Improved Pregnancy Outcome Program.* Tupelo, Miss.: Three Rivers District Health Department, Mississippi State Board of Health, 1980.

Smith, M. L., Glass, G. V., and Miller, T. I. *The Benefits of Psychotherapy.* Baltimore, Md.: Johns Hopkins University Press, 1980.

Thompson, M. S., and Meyer, H. J. "The Costs of AIDS: Alternative Methodological Approaches." In L. Sechrest, H. Freeman, and A. Mulley (eds.), *Health Services Research Methodology: A Focus on AIDS.* Publication No. (PHS) 89-3439. Rockville, Md.: National Center for Health Services Research and Health Care Technology Assessment, Public Health Service, U.S. Department of Health and Human Services, 1989.

Tukey, J. W. *Exploratory Data Analysis.* Reading, Mass.: Addison-Wesley, 1977.

Turner, C. F. *Public Perceptions and Behavior in Response to the AIDS Epidemic: Present Knowledge and Future Needs.* Unpublished manuscript, CBASSE Committee on AIDS Research, National Research Council, Washington, D.C., 1988.

Turner, C. F., Fay, R. E., and Widdus, R. *Monitoring the Spread of HIV Infection.* Unpublished manuscript, CBASSE Committee on AIDS Research, National Research Council, Washington, D.C., 1988.

Valdiserri, R. O., Lyter, D. W., Kingsley, L. A., Leviton, L. C., Schofield, J. W., Huggins, J., Ho, M., and Rinaldo, C. R. "The Effect of Group Education on Improving Attitudes About AIDS Risk Reduction." *New York State Journal of Medicine,* May 1987, pp. 272–278.

Valdiserri, R. O., Lyter, D. W., Leviton, L. C., Stoner, K., and Silvestre, A. *Applying the Criteria for the Development of Health Promotion and Education Programs to AIDS Risk Reduction Programs for Gay Men.* Unpublished manuscript, Graduate School of Public Health, University of Pittsburgh, 1988.

Watson, J. D. *The Double Helix.* New York: Atheneum, 1968.

Woolgar, S. (ed.). *Knowledge and Reflexivity: New Frontiers in the Sociology of Knowledge.* London: Sage, 1988.

Zwick, W. R., and Velicer, W. F. "Comparison of Five Rules for Determining the Number of Components to Retain." *Psychological Bulletin,* 1986, *99,* 432–442.

WILLIAM R. SHADISH is professor of psychology at Memphis State University. He is author (with Thomas D. Cook and Laura C. Leviton) of Foundations of Program Evaluation *and current editor of* New Directions for Program Evaluation.

*The validity of results generated within any individual study are
likely to be equivocal because of many threats to validity that cannot
be tested directly. Using meta-analysis, this chapter shows how it is
possible to examine, empirically, the influence of between-study
differences in research designs, measures, intervention strategies, and
contextual factors on various forms of validity of study results.*

Strengthening Causal Interpretations of Nonexperimental Data: The Role of Meta-analysis

David S. Cordray

Two paradoxical trends can be found in contemporary applied social
research. First, although several decades of social, behavioral, educational,
and medical research and evaluation have resulted in a growing stockpile
of published and unpublished studies, technical reviews generally reveal
that most impact studies suffer from methodological shortcomings. As a
consequence, inferences about what works are weakened. Second, as the
knowledge base has grown, technologies for summarizing the results of
past impact studies—most notably meta-analysis—have developed at a
rapid pace (Durlak and Lipsey, 1991). In particular, investigators seeking
to derive an efficient and comprehensive summary of prior research have
rediscovered, refined, and applied statistical methods for aggregating
evidence in a variety of applied social research areas (Cordray and Fischer,
in press).

Some researchers who are willing to embrace the concept of meta-
analysis worry that the quality of applied social research does not warrant
aggregation of the resulting data. This chapter shows how meta-analysis
can help to improve the quality of inference derived from nonexperimental
data. In doing so, it describes and illustrates meta-analysis—a family of

---

A version of this paper was published in L. Sechrest, E. Perrin, and J. Bunker (eds.),
Research Methodology: Strengthening Causal Interpretations of Nonexperimental Data.
Washington, D.C.: Agency for Health Care Policy and Research, Public Health Service,
U.S. Department of Health and Human Services, 1990.

© Jossey-Bass Publishers

statistical methods. It highlights the ways in which meta-analytic procedures can be improved, and it argues that meta-analysis procedures can
improve causal inference by helping us to understand the direction and
magnitude of the bias introduced by technical transgressions.

What Is Meta-analysis?

Meta-analysis involves a variety of statistical and nonstatistical methods
that can be used for reviewing and summarizing past research. It has many
uses, and it comes in a variety of forms. The diversity of meta-analytic
activities can be readily seen in the many textbooks and articles that are
currently available on the topic. Bangert-Drowns (1986) provides a history
of the development of meta-analytic methods. Durlak and Lipsey (1991)
offer a useful guide to meta-analytic procedures. And, other treatments, of
varying levels of technical discourse, are widely available (Cook and
others, 1992; Cooper, 1989; Cooper and Hedges, in press; Glass, McGaw,
and Smith, 1981; Hedges and Olkin, 1985; Hunter and Schmidt, 1990;
Light and Pillemer, 1984; Rosenthal, 1984; Slavin, 1986; U.S. General
Accounting Office, 1983, 1990; Wachter and Straf, 1990).

This chapter is concerned in particular with the ways in which the
outcomes and methodological features of past studies are handled as part
of the meta-analytic process. Some meta-analytic studies (Shakih, Vayda,
and Feldman, 1976) conduct quantitative analyses of research quality but
do not assess the effects of methodological quality on study outcomes.
Others (Kavale and Forness, 1983) perform quantitative analysis of outcomes but use qualitative procedures to treat design quality. If meta-
analysis is to improve the methodological quality of primary studies,
procedures that involve quantitative analysis of both outcomes and study
characteristics (Devine, 1992; Lipsey, 1992; Shadish, 1992) are the most
relevant. For that reason, this chapter highlights the statistical treatment of
study outcomes and characteristics.

Of course, the idea of combining results of independent studies statistically is not new. Stigler (1986) traces the history of quantitative aggregation. As Hedges and Olkin (1985) note, the statistical roots for modern
meta-analysis date back to the early 1930s, when methods for combining
probabilities resulting from statistical tests conducted across studies were
first developed. During the same period, Cochran (1937) developed procedures for combining numerical estimates of treatment effects. Although
the resulting statistical machinery has been available for several decades,
it was not applied on a large scale in the social and behavioral sciences until
the mid 1970s, when Glass (1976) introduced the concept of meta-
analysis. Since that time, hundreds of meta-analyses have been undertaken.
Durlak and Lipsey (1991) estimate that more than 600 meta-analyses have
been conducted since the mid 1970s.

Stages of the Meta-analytic Process

Operationally, meta-analytic methods are simple and appealing. Typically, six interdependent or conditional steps are involved. As with any research endeavor, the first step is to specify the questions of interest clearly. For example, the area of interest may be the therapeutic effects of alternative treatments for hypertension (for example, drugs versus weight-loss programs). The synthesis can have any one of several aims, ranging from simple aggregation of available study results with no between-study comparisons (Collins and Langman, 1985) to studies that undertake complex comparisons to improve our understanding of the differences among studies (Devine and Cook, 1983) and the explanatory mechanisms underlying causal hypotheses (Becker, 1992; Devine, 1992).

Each objective implies different meta-analytic practices. Depending on the scope of the questions that meta-analysis is to address, the second step—specifying the research domain—can include all studies, only those studies that are methodologically high in quality, or only high-quality studies that directly test alternative treatments. This second step is similar to delineating the population frame in survey research. That the choices made in these first two steps have an impact on the generalizability of results of a meta-analysis should be obvious. Moreover, front-end decisions to exclude studies based on preconceived notions about study quality can, as I argue later, seriously limit the amount of knowledge that we can derive about the effects of methodological transgressions.

The third step is to gather data for our meta-analysis. Here, the primary objective is to identify all relevant published and unpublished studies. The fourth step is possibly the most time-consuming: We must review each report that we obtain and extract information from it. Typically, we record three types of information: the primary results (for example, probability levels, test statistics) and derived summary statistics (for example, effect sizes), study methodology (for example, assignment rules, attrition levels, sample sizes, the measurement process, analysis, statistical power), and study characteristics (for example, contexts, participants, programmatic and theory-related dimensions).

The fifth step is to aggregate research results statistically. Besides techniques that allow us to derive an overall estimate of the effects of an intervention strategy across multiple independent assessments, we also need a variety of diagnostic and validation strategies. Hedges and Olkin (1985) and Rosenthal (Rosenthal, 1984; Rosenthal and Rubin, 1982) have demonstrated the statistical pitfalls of early practices and provided a firm statistical foundation for the aggregation of results. The sixth step is to present our results in ways that maximize the utility and clarity of our meta-analysis (Cooper, 1989; Light and Pillemer, 1984).

How Can Meta-analysis Improve Causal Inference?

For a variety of reasons—some valid, some not—meta-analysis has not met with universal acceptance. Among the valid reasons are concerns about the quality of the studies to be aggregated. Reviews of the methodological quality of past studies repeatedly observe that not all data are of equal inferential clarity (Lipsey, Crosse, Dunkle, and others, 1985). That is, the large number of low-quality studies immediately calls into question the wisdom of accumulating or combining their results. There are two obvious questions at this point: What value is there in combining poor studies? and How can meta-analysis improve causal inference from nonexperimental data?

Nonexperimental Results Are Not Always Biased. It is difficult to draw causal inferences about the effectiveness of interventions even under the best of circumstances. We tend to think that the risks of erroneous causal ascriptions are greater when nonexperimental data are involved than they are when the data are generated in well-controlled experimental designs, such as randomized clinical trials. However, methodological transgressions associated with nonexperimental designs generate only plausible rival explanations. They are not related to bias in the estimates of the magnitude of effects, and they should be treated as empirical propositions. In fact, direct comparison of results generated in quasi-experiments with results developed in randomized trials does not uniformly reveal differences that could be attributed to bias inherent in quasi-experiments. Boruch (1987) has several examples.

Moreover, the presence of bias in a study's estimates does not automatically render it useless. In many instances, the questions are, How big is the bias? and Would reliance on biased information lead to improper actions—for example, would it lead us to prescribe or follow a treatment regimen that in fact was harmful? The statistical framework underlying meta-analysis gives us a way of systematically examining the presence, direction, and magnitude of bias introduced by the methodological features of past studies. We can often control for the influence of bias statistically (Cook and others, 1992).

Enhancing Statistical Power. One problem noted in methodological reviews of past studies is low statistical power. That is, they do not enable us to detect a treatment effect even if it is present. There are three principal reasons: small sample sizes, insufficient evidence on the likely magnitude of the effect, and insensitive outcome measures. By combining results from high-quality studies, meta-analysis can enhance statistical power. As one of the meta-analyses discussed in the next section shows, this enhancement is not always achieved (Collins and Langman, 1985).

Improving Generalization. Even well-controlled studies are subject to inferential limitations. For example, they may not allow us to generalize over time, persons, treatment operationalizations, or settings. Although statistical aggregation of results across studies does not free us from the logical problems of induction, it does give us an empirical footing that helps us to judge the likely generalizability of findings. To date, meta-analysts have not routinely engaged in practices that shed light on the generalizability issue, except through statistical reasoning.

Improving Subsequent Planning. Even if we decide that all past assessments are insufficient, meta-analysis can help us to plan future studies. I have argued (Cordray and Orwin, 1983; Cordray and Sonnefeld, 1985) that such by-products of meta-analysis as study attributes can be used to obtain reality-based estimates of critical study dimensions. For example, synthesis of methodological features underlying psychological intervention before surgery reveals that sample sizes are typically smaller than thirty per group and rarely more than 100. These numbers may reflect poor planning or natural constraints on the patient pool. If natural constraints are the reason, subsequent studies may need to consider other ways of improving the statistical sensitivity of the assessment (Cordray and Sonnefeld, 1985; Lipsey, 1990).

Limitations of Meta-analysis. Like other strategies for strengthening causal inference—for example, causal modeling—meta-analysis is subject to the very problems that it tries to circumvent. That is, although meta-analysis gives us a statistical framework for combining results of studies and examining the influence of the kinds of flaws associated with nonexperimental data, it is also subject to inferential errors arising from the observational (read *nonexperimental*) nature of its basic elements, namely study results. Even when all study results have been generated by well-executed experimental designs, moving beyond simple statistical aggregation of results to examine why studies produce different estimates of the magnitude of effects opens us to inferential errors, because all between-study comparisons are nonexperimental (Leamer, 1978).

Meta-analysis may also be limited in the sense that it is out of step with other advances in applied social research. The persistent uncertainty associated with nonexperimental assessments of causality has resulted in a variety of suggestions for reform. For some, causal modeling (Bentler, 1989; Rindskopf, 1986) and theory-driven approaches (Chen, 1990; Chen and Rossi, 1983; Cordray, 1986) are promising avenues for improvement. Under the flag of critical multiplism, Shadish, Cook, and Houts (1986) argue that any single design, approach, or perspective has inherent frailties. They advocate selecting several options that have biases in different directions. These new directions for primary studies suggest that future nonexperimental assessments will rely increasingly on sophisticated design, analysis, theory, and logic. Efforts to combine the results of individual studies are likely to become increasingly difficult as methodologies become more sophisticated or diversified.

Statistical Foundations for Meta-analysis

This section focuses on the fifth step of the meta-analysis process, aggregating research results statistically. As Cooper (1989) has noted, meta-analysis can be viewed as a special case of the more general notion of literature review. However, meta-analysis differs from the general notion in emphasizing the statistical treatment of study outcomes and characteristics. Since the technical aspects of meta-analysis do not have the same commonsense features as traditional literature reviews, it seems appropriate to highlight the core concepts. Nonstatistical issues and specialized statistical procedures are discussed in later sections.

The following example will help to introduce the statistical foundations of meta-analysis. Suppose that the effects of providing home health care have been investigated twelve times in the past ten years. Suppose further that the hypothetical data displayed in Table 3.1 represent the primary results of these investigations. As Table 3.1 shows, five of the twelve test statistics show differences larger than we would expect by chance. In four cases, home health care has a positive effect on indicators of functional status. In the fifth case, it has the opposite effect, which suggests that home health care is detrimental. The findings of the other studies are nonsignificant by conventional statistical standards. What conclusion can we draw from this collection of evidence? Is home health care effective?

If we simply count the positive, negative, and neutral tests of statistical significance, our answer has to be no. However, if we are concerned only with whether differences exceed an arbitrary probability value, we ignore a lot of information. Inspection of Table 3.1 reveals numerous differences across studies. For example, the means for individual studies hint that different instruments were used to measure outcomes. Moreover, some studies seem to have used homogeneous clients, while others did not. Each of these study characteristics could have an influence on study outcomes. Further, the decision rule on the presence or absence of treatment effect is quite crude. For example, two studies (3 and 4) approach statistical significance. If their samples had been larger, the results might have met conventional criteria. If the statistical criterion were adjusted downward (say, to $p < .1$) or if we argued after the fact that only one-tailed tests had any interest, six of the twelve studies would support the claim that the intervention had been effective. Still, is the cup half full or half empty? The data support either conclusion. Meta-analysis offers an alternative to this simple vote-counting tactic for determining overall effectiveness.

Table 3.1. Sample Sizes, Means, Pooled Standard
Deviations, and *t*-statistics for Twelve Hypothetical
Outcome Studies

Study	Sample Size		Mean		Standard Deviation	Test Statistic
	N^E	N^C	Y^E	Y^C	S^P	t
1	20	25	12	14	4.28	-1.56
2	20	25	6	5.5	2.00	.83
3	20	25	12	10	3.54	1.78
4	20	20	6	5	2.00	1.67
5	25	20	14	10	3.90	3.42*
6	25	20	5.5	5	2.00	.83
7	400	380	29.5	25	11.02	5.70*
8	25	25	95	65	22.64	4.69*
9	25	25	12	10	5.00	1.42
10	25	25	7	6.5	4.77	1.00
11	100	100	10	12	3.76	-3.77*
12	10	15	30	20	4.00	3.76*

*$p < .05$; one-tailed.

Some Statistical Aspects of Meta-analysis. In his original description of meta-analysis, Glass (1976) suggested that we can generate a meaningful summary of the collective results of studies, even if they differ in their way of measuring outcomes, by transforming findings into a common metric fashioned after Cohen's *d* statistic. This metric has been labeled *effect size* and represented as *g*. Glass (1976) represented the effect size as the standardized difference between means of experimental ($\overline{Y^E}$) and control ($\overline{Y^C}$) conditions. That is,

$$g = \frac{(\overline{Y^E} - \overline{Y^C})}{(S_p)}$$

where S_p is the pooled standard deviation. Under Glass's (1976) original conception of meta-analysis, the combined effect of the intervention across studies was a simple arithmetic average of all effect sizes. For the hypothetical data on the effects of home health care shown in Table 3.1, the average effect size is .54. That is, on average, the functional status of participants in the experimental treatment (home health care) exceeds that of participants in the control condition (normal care) by slightly more than one-half of a standard deviation. Applying the logic of standard statistical hypothesis testing, we find that the average effect size is significantly different from zero ($t[11]=2.35$, $p < .01$). Although only four studies show the experimental treatment as having had a positive effect on functional status, in the aggregate, the twelve studies show that the intervention is effective.

Rosenthal (1984) summarizes an alternative method for aggregating results across multiple studies. Rather than transforming the between-group means into a common metric, as Glass (1976) does, Rosenthal refers to the early statistical literature on the combining of probabilities. A variety of methods are applicable under certain restrictions (Rosenthal, 1984). One common technique entails transforming the exact probability reported for a between-group difference into its corresponding Z value in a standard normal distribution. The summary calculation across studies is the following:

$$Z_C = \frac{\sum_{i=1}^{N} Z_{pi}}{\sqrt{N}}$$

The probability of Z_c is viewed as the likelihood of the combined effects of the treatment across assessments. Z_{pi} is the normal deviate for each probability p in study i. N is simply the number of probability values included in the synthesis. For the hypothetical data shown in Table 3.1, the combined Z_c is 5.2 ($p < .001$). As with the average effect size, the aggregate effects of treatment are statistically reliable even though the results of only four studies exceed the conventional statistical criterion.

The primary reason for using these transformations is that measures and measurement levels (for example, dichotomous versus continuous measures) may differ from one study to the next. When measures differ, the interpretation of effect size can be difficult because of differential sensitivity and relevance of measures to treatment. With the exception of a few knotty issues concerning the appropriateness and meaning of the transformation (Sechrest and Yeaton, 1982), the foregoing is elementary and very straightforward in cases where research quality is consistently high across studies (for example, in simple experiments where individual estimates are unbiased). Meta-analysis becomes more complicated when studies differ in elegance, quality, or type of design used. There are at least two ways in which we can accommodate such differences: We can exclude the studies that fail to achieve acceptable levels of quality, or we can retain them and weight their findings in accordance with our judgment of their elegance, quality, and so on. Rosenthal (1984) suggests that the summary calculation would assume the following form if a weighting factor were applied:

$$Z'_C = \frac{\sum_{i=1}^{N} (W_i Z_{pi})}{\sqrt{\sum W_i^2}}$$

This calculation would obtain the combined probability for Z'_c not for Z_c as earlier. Use of a quality rating ranging from 1 (low) to 10 (high) to weight the hypothetical data (see "w_i" under "Combined Probabilities" in Table 3.2) yields a combined Z'_c of 4.7 (that is, $79.91 \sqrt{291}$). Although the weighted Z is smaller than the unweighted Z, it is still statistically reliable.

The statistical logic of Rosenthal's (1984) procedures for combining probabilities is clear. And the statistical properties of the effect size measure have been extensively investigated and elaborated in recent years. Hedges and Olkin (1985) argue that appropriate statistical practices for meta-analysis must consider sampling error in primary study estimates and models of the differences underlying studies. These issues are summarized later in this chapter. As the reader will note, they are not trivial in the sense that the results of meta-analysis can be influenced considerably by the statistical procedures that we use.

Hedges and Olkin (1985) argue that early meta-analysis failed to take sampling error into account, and they have offered a different framework for the aggregation of study results. Their statistical rationale is quite simple. The parameter of interest in meta-analysis is the population effect size

$$\delta = \frac{\mu^E - \mu^C}{\sigma^P}$$

Table 3.2. Basic Transformations for Effect Sizes and Significance Levels for Twelve Hypothetical Studies

	Effect Size				Combined Probabilities			
Study	d_i	w_i	$w_i d_i$	$w_i d_i^2$	Z	w_i	Zw_i	w_i^2
1	-.462	10.8167	-4.9757	2.2888	-1.51	1	-1.51	1
2	2.46	11.2657	2.8164	.7041	.82	4	3.28	16
3	.549	9.6358	5.2997	2.9148	1.72	6	10.32	36
4	.490	9.7087	4.7573	2.3311	1.63	2	3.26	4
5	.982	9.9334	9.7347	9.5400	3.00	1	3.00	1
6	.246	11.0266	2.7567	.6892	.82	4	3.28	16
7	.410	191.2046	78.3939	32.1415	5.00*	2	10.00	4
8	1.309	10.2923	13.4829	17.6626	4.00*	8	32.00	64
9	.394	12.2669	4.7841	1.8658	1.37	10	13.70	100
10	.276	12.393	3.4662	.9705	.98	6	5.88	36
11	-.528	48.3092	-25.6039	13.5701	-3.40	3	-10.20	9
12	2.410	3.5357	8.5210	20.5357	3.40	2	6.80	4
Total		340.3749	103.4333	105.2142	17.83		79.91	291

*approximated

where μ^E, μ^C, and σ^P are population parameters corresponding to the mean of the treatment group (μ^E), the mean of the control groups (μ^C), and the pooled standard deviation (σ^P). As such, each estimate of δ contains two sources of variation:

$$g_i = \delta + \varepsilon$$

δ represents systematic variation of g, and ε represents sampling error.

Further, Glass's (1976) estimator for effect size is biased when sample sizes are small. We can correct for the effects of this bias by the use of simple adjustment to g:

$$d_i = g_i 1 - \left[\frac{3}{4n^E + 4n^c - 9}\right]$$

To differentiate the corrected estimate of effect size (g_i) from the uncorrected estimate (g), Hedges and Olkin (1985) designate the corrected estimate as d_i. The correction has a notable effect on estimates of effect size when samples are small (less than fifty), and it vanishes as the sample size increases beyond fifty. For the hypothetical data, the correction has a minor effect on the simple arithmetic average of effect sizes. The .52 that it yields contrasts little with the .54 reported for g.

One way in which meta-analysis departs from conventional statistical applications for primary studies concerns the estimation of error variance and how it treats this variance as part of the aggregation process. According to Hedges (Hedges, 1981, 1982, 1984; Hedges and Olkin, 1985), if the t or F test that the primary researchers used is valid, the variance of d is completely determined by the sample sizes and the value of d. As such, it is possible to determine the sampling variance of d from a single observation:

$$y = \frac{n^E + n^c}{n^E + n^C} + \frac{d^2}{2(n^E + n^C)}$$

Further, Hedges and Olkin (1985) show that the most precise way of combining results involves a weighted average that takes into account the variance of each d. As such, the average effect size ($d.$) is derived as follows:

$$d. = \sum_{i=1}^{k} w_i d_i / \sum_{i=1}^{k} w_i$$

where

$$w_i = 1/v_i$$

or

$$w_i = \frac{2(n_i^E + n_i^C)\, n_i^E n_i^C}{2(n_i^E + n_i^C)^2 + n_i^E n_i^C d_i^2}$$

Applying the Hedges and Olkin (1985) framework to the hypothetical data set (see Table 3.2), the weighted average effect size (103.43/340.37) is .30. That is, rather than the one-half of a standard deviation reported earlier, the difference is now about one-third of a standard deviation.

When it can be assumed that the k studies share a common population value (δ), the weighted mean for d is approximately normal, with a mean of δ and variance of

$$V. = 1/\sum_{i-1}^{k} W_i$$

Applied to the hypothetical data, the aggregate effect size is statistically different from zero ($Z = 5.3$, $p < .001$). That is, $Z = .30/.056 = 5.3$, with a 95 percent confidence interval of +.19 to +.41.

Examination of the individual d_i values in Table 3.2 shows that the weighted average masks substantial variability between studies. A major question for meta-analysts concerns the reasons for these differences. For the hypothetical data, Table 3.3 enumerates some factors that many investigators

Table 3.3. Study, Population, and Treatement Characteristics for Twelve Hypothetical Outcome Studies

	Study Characteristics						
Study	Year of Publication	Random Assignment	Adequate Measures	Treatment Implementation	Quality Score	Client	Treatment Setting
1	early	no	no	low	1	adults	clinic
2	early	yes	yes	low	4	children	home
3	late	yes	no	high	6	children	hospital
4	late	no	yes	high	2	adults	clinic
5	late	no	no	low	1	adults	hospital
6	early	no	yes	high	4	children	school
7	early	no	no	high	2	children	clinic
8	late	yes	no	high	8	adults	hospital
9	late	yes	yes	high	10	children	hospital
10	late	yes	yes	low	6	adults	clinic
11	early	no	no	low	3	children	school
12	late	no	no	low	2	children	clinic

suspect to be related to the magnitude of effect size. These factors include random assignment to treatments, adequacy of measures, and degree of treatment implementation. Table 3.3 also reports the same overall quality score used in the weighted Z procedure. Client characteristics and treatment settings are other sources of noncompatibilities. Such heterogeneity among studies is quite normal for meta-analysis. Two questions can be raised: To what extent do these substantive and methodological differences between studies account for the heterogeneity in estimates of d? and How generalizable are the results? To the extent that d's are homogeneous and conditions are heterogeneous, we may consider the results to be generalizable within the boundaries established by the conditions represented by the studies. Moreover, these heterogeneity formulas enable us to determine whether differences between studies in design quality have any relation to their outcomes (the effect size)—a result that moves the issue of whether the results are due to rival explanations onto empirical ground. Even if we find that methodological artifacts explain some treatment effects, the statistical machinery of meta-analysis gives us a way of controlling for these effects. Lipsey (1992) and Shadish (1992) provide detailed examples of the application of multivariate procedures in assessments of the influence of method artifacts.

The Hedges and Olkin (1985) framework provides a test for homogeneity of d_i's. This is given as

$$H_T = \sum_{i}^{k} W_i d_i^2 - \left(\sum_{i}^{k} W_i d_i \right)^2 / \left(\sum_{i}^{k} w_i \right)$$

and is used to determine if d's share a common δ. Homogeneity (H_T) can be tested in an approximate way by chi-square with $k-1$ degrees of freedom. Rosenthal and Rubin (1982) also provide a test for homogeneity of effect sizes and combined probabilities.

Hedges and Olkin (1985) show that H_T can be partitioned into between-study (H_B) differences and within-cluster (H_W) differences. That is,

$$H_T = H_B + H_{W,}$$

where $H_W = \Sigma H_{wj}$ or $H_W = H_{W1} + H_{W2} + \ldots + H_{wj}$ and $H_B = \Sigma W_{j.} (d_{j.}\text{-d..})^2$

H_{Wi} can be tested by chi-square with $k-p$ degrees of freedom, and H_B can be tested by chi-square with $p-1$ degrees of freedom.

The homogeneity test shows that the d's in the hypothetical data base do not share a common population parameter ($\chi^2[11] = 73.8$). That a study used random assignment to conditions reduced the chi-square by about 5 percent ($\chi^2[10]$ = 70.2) from the chi-square for total heterogeneity. Publication year (early versus late) reduced the chi-square by 27 percent, and several other tests of the separate effects of these factors produced marginal improvements in the goodness of fit. The overall quality rating—one that assumes a linear relationship among factors—did not account for the heterogeneity. In contrast, the closest fit was achieved by considering a three-way breakdown involving design x measurement quality x implementation level. Here, the value ($\chi^2[4]$ = 11.1) approached nonsignificance. Despite the fact that it was not possible to derive a model accounting for all the within-group variability in d's, it is interesting that this three-way breakdown reduced heterogeneity by 85 percent.

Summary. The preceding paragraphs have summarized the statistical features of meta-analysis and reviewed some state-of-the-art techniques for the quantitative combining of results. When Sechrest and Yeaton (1982, p. 579) reviewed the technical features of effect size measures, they concluded that many depended largely on "intuitions buttressed by some empirical norms." Although their conclusion still holds, the fact that we now have a fully developed statistical framework seems to have removed some of the need for intuition.

The preceding overview has addressed only a limited domain of meta-analysis. Others (for example, Finsterbusch, 1984; Hunter and Schmidt, 1990) have developed frameworks for the accumulation of correlational evidence; Hedges and Olkin (1985) discuss practices for combining a variety of other summary statistics, such as proportions; Cook and others (1992) describe the use of explanatory meta-analytic tactics; and the forthcoming *Handbook of Research Synthesis* (Cooper and Hedges, 1994) covers the latest advances in statistical and nonstatistical meta-analytic practices.

Even with these advances, intuition and good sense are still essential if meta-analysis is to be useful. The mechanical application of statistical techniques is not likely to yield results that are easy to interpret. Understanding the differences that we can observe in studies, the underlying methodologies, the historical context within which they were conducted, and the substantive issues of the area under investigation is a necessary part of the meta-analysis process. Finally, like all statistical procedures, meta-analytic tactics depend on assumptions that may or may not be true in a given application.

Despite some important analytic advances that have taken place in recent years, the exchange between Schmidt, Hunter, Pearlman, and Hirsh (1985) and Sackett, Schmitt, Tenopyr, and others (1985) shows that many statistical and nonstatistical issues remain the focus of considerable concern. The next section of this chapter summarizes seven recent meta-analyses.

Meta-analysis in Health Services, Medicine, and Surgery

In an early *Annual Review of Public Health,* Louis, Fineberg, and Mosteller (1985) reviewed the contributions of meta-analysis to the public health literature and uncovered several dozen papers on various aspects of meta-analysis. This section reviews some sets of meta-analyses to suggest how meta-analytic tactics can improve the quality of inference in nonexperimental data.

Coronary Artery Bypass Graft Surgery. Wortman and Yeaton (1983) synthesized the results of twenty-five studies on the effects of coronary artery bypass graft surgery or nonsurgical interventions on coronary artery disease. Their analysis included results from nine randomized clinical trials and sixteen controlled trials that had not employed random assignment—quasi-experiments. They selected these studies from a list of ninety studies culled from literature reviews, references in articles selected for synthesis, and a MEDLARS II search of studies appearing between 1970 and 1978. They did not consider studies that did not include evidence on mortality or survival rates. They also rejected studies that did not use a control group (that is, preexperimental designs, such as case studies) and studies employing historical controls. Their rationale for the last decision was that Sacks, Chalmers, and Smith (1982) had already demonstrated that historical controls consistently overestimated the effectiveness of bypass surgery.

Wortman and Yeaton (1983) used several procedures to aggregate the effects of these treatments. They calculated differences in survival and mortality rates, along with averages for each study and computed an effect size–like indicator. Throughout the analysis, they presented results separately for randomized clinical trials and quasi-experiments. Differences in survival and mortality rates between surgical and medical interventions were, on average, 4 to 5 percent for the randomized clinical trials. For quasi-experiments, mortality and survival rates were, on average, respectively 14 and 24 percentage points lower. The effect size–like indicator— an aggregated mean difference divided by the standard deviation of the differences—showed effects of 0.75 and 1.0 for survival rates stemming from randomized clinical trials and quasi-experiments, respectively. For mortality, the effect sizes were about 0.80 regardless of the design.

These aggregate figures mask a substantial amount of variability among studies within each group. The authors did not conduct homogeneity tests. Table 3.4 clearly shows that data generated by quasi-experimental designs were more variable than data stemming from randomized clinical trials.

In attempting to explain why the average benefits of surgery appear to be higher for quasi-experiments than they seem to be for randomized clinical trials, Wortman and Yeaton (1983) conducted a series of between-study comparisons. Their additional analyses of such factors as differential severity of patient conditions, crossovers, recency of trial, and changes in the composition of the patient population suggest that several important sampling, design, and treatment characteristics confounded between-study (or cluster) comparisons.

Table 3.4. Distribution of Percentage Differences Between Surgical and Nonsurgical Interventions for Survival and Mortality Indicators

Percentage Difference	Outcome	
	Survival	Mortality
+40	QQ	Q
+35		Q
+30	QQ	
+25	Q	Q
	Q	QQ
+20	Q	
+15		QQQ
	•Q	•
+10	••	••
		••QQ
+5		
0	•Q	•
-5	••	Q
		Q
-10	Q	
		Q
-15		Q
-20		

Note: •=randomized clinical trial; Q=quasi-experiment.
Source: Wortman and Yeaton (1983).

Aphasia Therapy. Aphasia is a condition in which an individual's ability to interpret and formulate language symbols is impaired, he or she loses the ability to decode and encode linguistic elements, and other intellectual functioning is impaired. It is typically the result of a cerebrovascular accident (that is, a stroke), trauma, neoplasms, or infection. Language therapy has been widely practiced and tested as a rehabilitative strategy. Research strategies have been heterogeneous, and results of studies on the effectiveness of aphasia therapy have been mixed. Greenhouse and others (1990) use meta-analytic procedures to answer the question, Does aphasia therapy work?

Focusing on a subset of thirteen studies employing a pre- and posttreatment design with patients observed approximately three months after their stroke (to control for spontaneous recovery), Greenhouse and others (1990) found an average effect size of .80 (95 percent confidence interval = .50, 1.10) or 1.37 (95 percent confidence interval = .73, 2.03), depending on how effect size had been defined. Results weighted by sample size were roughly comparable. Although the investigators did not conduct a test of homogeneity, they did perform several diagnostic assessments, which showed that their results were robust relative to the file-drawer problem (that is, their inability to obtain all studies), imputation for missing data, and chance variation (although they treated each study as a single data point).

Psychological Interventions and Recovery from Surgery and Heart Attacks. Researchers have documented that psychological factors can influence health status and utilization of health services. Two meta-analyses assessed the effects of psychological interventions on recovery from surgery and heart attacks. The first, by Mumford, Schlesinger, and Glass (1982), examined effects of psychological interventions across many different outcomes. The second, by Devine and Cook (1983), refined their analysis by focusing on effects of psychoeducational treatments on length of hospital stay and examining five threats to validity.

Mumford, Schlesinger, and Glass (1982) used a MEDLARS search and an inspection of key references in the literature (1955–1978) on psychological support as an adjunct to medical services to locate thirty-four controlled studies. Among them, these studies provided 210 estimates of effect size across ten categories of outcomes (for example, self-ratings of pain, cooperation with treatment, speed of recovery, length of hospital stay). According to these analysts, psychotherapeutic approaches produced an average effect size of 0.41, slightly higher than the 0.30 found for educational approaches. Combined approaches were superior to either alone (0.65).

These researchers also reviewed a subset of ten studies that had examined the effects of these interventions on length of hospital stay, an especially important outcome from the perspective of health care costs. They reported an average effect size of 0.25. When means of the ten studies were weighted by sample size and size of the standard deviation (consistent with Hedges and Olkin, 1985), these investigators found that length of hospital stay was about 2.4 days fewer for patients receiving preoperative psychotherapeutic interventions than it was for standard surgical procedures. This difference was statistically reliable.

Effects of Psychoeducational Interventions on Length of Hospital Stay. As just noted, Devine and Cook (1983) extended the literature search conducted by Mumford, Schlesinger, and Glass (1982) to MEDLARS (1974–1981), *Dissertation Abstracts* (1961–1981), and *Psychological Abstracts* (1967–1981), a tactic that yielded more than a hundred studies on the effects of psychoeducation interventions on length of hospital stay. Of that number, thirty-four studies met Devine and Cook's (1983) inclusion criteria. In conducting their quantitative review, these investigators calculated effect sizes when possible, and, since the outcome measure of interest, length of hospital stay, was roughly comparable across investigations, they also reported a percentage difference for each study. Analyses were based on two different units of analysis: studies and comparisons. That is, some studies reported multiple comparisons, due to multiple measures on the same groups, to multiple groups, or to follow-up testing.

As already noted, Mumford, Schlesinger, and Glass (1982) found an effect size of 0.25 for length of hospital stay on ten studies. The analysis of thirty-four studies by Devine and Cook (1983) yielded an average effect size—0.49 for studies and 0.48 for comparisons—that nearly doubled the previous value. However, their analysis of length of hospital stay revealed an average decline of about 1.2 to 1.6 days, depending on unit of analysis, studies or comparisons, and average percentage differences of 16 percent for studies and 13.4 percent for comparisons, somewhat less impressive than the results reported by Mumford, Schlesinger, and Glass (1982).

After partitioning the population of studies into subsets, Devine and Cook (1983) concluded that the relationship between interventions and decreased length of hospital stay did not depend on publication bias, when the study had been published, physician awareness of treatment assignment, subject assignment, or level of internal validity. "Because of this, we can be all the more confident that the interventions discussed probably do shorten hospital stays" (Devine and Cook, 1983, p. 427). When placebo conditions are used as the comparison group, the effect is smaller. However, noting the diversity of placebo conditions (Cordray and Bootzin, 1983), Devine and Cook (1983) ruled out the possibility that reduced length of hospital stay could be attributed to a Hawthorne effect.

They explained the differences between their results and those obtained by Mumford, Schlesinger, and Glass (1982) as attributable to differences in the number of studies included; differing decisions rules on the inclusion of specific studies; and increased diversity in types of surgery, patients, modes of treatment delivery, and caregivers between the two sets of studies.

Effects of Weight-Loss Treatments on Hypertension. Hypertension—that is, blood pressure chronically above 140/90 mmHg—increases the risk of cardiovascular disease and mortality. A variety of pharmacological and nonpharmacological treatments or treatment components have been prescribed to control or reduce hypertension. Hovell's (1982) meta-analysis examines the effects of one nonpharmacological procedure, weight loss, for decreasing blood pressure. This author reviewed twenty-one intervention studies and rated them for design quality and measurement characteristics. The rating scheme served as the basis for identifying the studies that could be most trusted for assessing the effects of weight loss on hypertension.

Hovell (1982) determined that six of the twenty-one studies were sufficiently sound methodologically to provide reasonable numerical estimates. Using evidence from the intervention conditions in these six studies, the author concluded that average systolic blood pressure was reduced by 21mmHg, average diastolic blood pressure declined by 13mmHg, and average weight loss was reduced by about 12 kilograms. Since the control groups also showed a reduction in each measure, Hovell's (1982) estimates of average effects are overstated. A simple reanalysis of the available evidence shows that the average changes were -17.6 mmHg, -10.9 mmHg, and -8.2 kgs, respectively. These values differ from Hovell's (1982) for two reasons: Information was not available for the control groups in two of the six studies for both measures of blood pressure (one study did not have information on weight loss for the control group), and the intervention and control conditions were contrasted before the individual results were aggregated.

Effects of Diet on Hyperactivity. Kavale and Forness (1983) identified, reviewed, and quantitatively synthesized twenty-three controlled studies examining the effects of a diet modification advocated by Benjamin Feingold (1975) as a treatment for hyperactivity. The intervention was designed to eliminate all food containing natural salicylates and artificial food additives from the diet.

An unspecified literature search strategy produced twenty-five studies. Twenty-three included control groups. All studies had been published, either in journals or in books. Together they yielded a total of 125 effect size measurements.

When Kavale and Forness (1983) used the study as the unit of analysis, the mean effect size was 0.02, with a 95 percent confidence interval of -.18 to .22. When effect size was used as the unit of analysis, the average was about 0.12, (CI = .05, .19). In a subsequent analysis, Kavale and Forness argued that differential reactivity of measures and inadequacy of research designs accounted for most of the effect. That is, while the average effect size for nonreactive measures was roughly zero, reactive measures, on average, produced an effect size of 0.18. The methodologically strongest research designs had an average effect size of .05 (CI = -.05, .14). The authors concluded that the literature did not support the Feingold intervention.

Effects of Histamine H_2 Antagonists in Acute Upper Gastrointestinal Hemorrhage. Collins and Langman (1985) noted that there had been twenty-seven randomized trials of the effects of histamine H_2 antagonists on acute upper gastrointestinal hemorrhage (that is, bleeding ulcers) but that none had been sufficiently large to provide statistically reliable evidence on three major endpoints: persistent or recurrent bleeding, need for surgery, and death. For this reason, they statistically combined the available evidence from published and unpublished randomized controlled trials. They identified trials through manual and computerized literature searches, reference lists, and discussions with colleagues and manufacturers of the H_2 antagonists. Rather than effect sizes, they used typical odds ratios (Mantel and Haenszel, 1959) as summary statistics. Further, following the Hedges and Olkin (1985) logic, the authors conducted tests of statistical significance and tested for homogeneity.

The combined analysis included more than 2,500 patients. Typical odds ratios of 0.89 (with a 95 percent confidence interval of .73 to 1.08), 0.78 (with a 95 percent confidence interval of .61 to 1.00), and 0.70 (with a 95 percent confidence interval of .50 to .96) were reported for bleeding, need for surgery, and death, respectively. As the confidence intervals show, the effects were not statistically reliable for persistent or recurrent bleeding, and they were marginally significant for the other two outcomes. However, inspection of data partitioned by site of ulcer (gastric or duodenal) suggested that benefits were confined to the gastric site. In contrast to most of the other meta-analysts whose work is discussed here, Collins and Langman (1985) took a dim view of post hoc breakdowns. They referred to such findings as *suggestive* and called for a large-scale prospective randomized trial.

Summary. The meta-analyses just reviewed illustrate the ways in which meta-analysis has been applied in health services research, medicine, and surgery. These examples show how the effects of plausible rival explanations can be probed across studies. They also show that decisions to exclude studies with poor methodological features limit what we can learn from meta-analysis. And they illustrate the steps involved in meta-analysis. Although the preceding examples all come from the public health literature, most of the issues with which they deal are general and apply to meta-analyses in a variety of areas.

The examples also show considerable variation in the conduct of meta-analysis, variation observed even when several syntheses purport to have the same general aim. Some of these differences arise from the fact that the technology for meta-analysis had been developing rapidly during the years in which these syntheses were conducted. Moreover, setting aside the rather crude and sometimes haphazard way in which meta-analytic studies combine and test results, we can note that many simple nonstatistical practices, such as study identification, raise questions about the accuracy and validity of past meta-analyses. The next section considers meta-analytic practices in more detail.

Assessing Practices

If all primary studies were well executed, adequately reported, and routinely available in the public domain, meta-analysis would be largely a technical exercise of converting findings into a common metric, such as effect size; applying the appropriate aggregation rules; and testing for homogeneity of results. In practice, the nature of the data that are available does not permit us to apply meta-analytic tactics mechanically. Each application requires a certain amount of adaptation and problem solving as well as numerous judgment calls. The question becomes, On what grounds can the adequacy of these practices be judged?

Several criteria can be postulated. At the most abstract level, conventional standards of quality (for example, Evaluation Research Society, 1982) could be applied. This level seems justified by the fact that, although some aspects of meta-analysis, such as the standardization of results into a common metric, are unique, there is no compelling reason for judging meta-analytic practices on grounds different from those used to judge other methods. From the standpoint of this rather abstract concept of quality, meta-analysts should aspire to produce results that are accurate, valid, and well enough documented that others can replicate their procedures. Further, general standards prescribe that assumptions should be clearly identified, evidence should be presented in defense of critical methodological choices, and generalization of results should be appropriate. Judging whether a particular study meets these criteria invokes a second level of assessment, namely, an examination of the specific features of the meta-analytic task.

Given that meta-analysis is a cluster of methodologies, it is not surprising that its practices closely resemble those of other research strategies, such as survey research. Inasmuch as the vulnerabilities of these other strategies have been systematically examined, it seems useful to draw on them when assessing meta-analysis practices. One framework that holds some promise is Kish's (1965) general model of total survey error. If we apply his concepts to synthesis practices, it becomes evident that there are several possible sources both of variable (that is, random) error and several sources of systematic error (that is, bias). The literature on meta-analysis (Rosenthal, 1984; Sacks and others, 1987) has already identified some of these. Although the concept of total survey error is not exactly congruent with issues in meta-analysis, it does provide a meaningful heuristic for organizing the issues that have and have not been examined.

Variable Errors. Variable errors can occur in two forms: as sampling errors and as other errors. Sampling errors, which must be distinguished from sampling bias, have an expectation of zero. Other errors can arise from the interjection of noise into the data-processing phase or from data collection procedures (that is, coding).

Sampling Errors. Sampling error in primary studies is an obvious source of random error. Hedges and Olkin (1985) have treated it in detail. Their formulation, which decomposes systematic and nonsystematic sources of variability as part of the aggregation process, serves as the foundation for testing of statistical significance and ascertaining the degree of heterogeneity within and across clusters of studies (Hedges, 1984). Only two studies— Collins and Langman (1985) and Mumford, Schlesinger, and Glass (1982)— modeled these components explicitly. The other meta-analyses established sampling variability by treating each effect size as a data point and applying conventional statistical techniques, which in all likelihood are underpowered when studies are the unit of analysis or inappropriate when multiple effect sizes within studies are the unit of analysis (because effect sizes are not independent). Sacks and others (1987) reported that 66 percent of the meta-analyses they reviewed used adequate statistical procedures.

Processing Errors. Other forms of variable error arise from nonsampling sources at both levels of analysis. A seemingly trivial set of errors can occur in connection with routine data processing (for example, errors in data entry). These errors can have profound effects on primary analyses as well as on meta-analyses. Rosenthal (1984) reports on twenty-seven studies that investigated a variety of recording errors in primary studies; these ranged from 1 to more than

40 percent. (Some recording errors appear to be the result of variable error. Others suggest bias in the direction of confirming the investigator's hypothesis.) However, none of the meta-analyses examined in the preceding section reported any irregularities in the primary data, despite the probability that they occur quite often (Trochim and Visco, 1985; Wolins, 1962). Unfortunately, there is very little evidence on the pervasiveness of processing errors.

Coding Errors. Variable error due to unreliability of coding and transcription can be substantial, and it can occur at both primary and meta-analytic levels. Only one study—Hovell (1982)—considered the reliability of outcome measures at the level of primary studies, and none of the meta-analyses considered the reliability of their own coding of outcomes and study characteristics. According to Sacks and others (1987), only 5 percent of the meta-analyses that they reviewed had performed tests of interrater agreement; 10 percent had performed partial assessments.

To underline the importance of coding errors at the meta-analytic level, I can point to a reanalysis (Orwin and Cordray, 1985) of a subset of the Smith, Glass, and Miller (1980) psychotherapy data base, which found that, depending on the type of variable that was being recorded, interrater agreement ranged from .40 to 1.0 (Table 3.5). Moreover, since there is no accepted method for

Table 3.5. Reliability Estimates for Smith, Glass, and Miller (1980) Psychotherapy Meta-analysis

Variable	Alternative Estimates		
	1	2	3
Diagnosis: neurotic, phobic, or depressive	0.98	0.98	0.89
Diagnosis: delinquent, felon, or habitué	1.00	1.00	1.00
Diagnosis: psychotic	1.00	1.00	1.00
Clients self-presented	0.97	0.57	0.71
Clients solicited	0.93	0.86	0.81
Individual therapy	1.00	1.00	0.85
Group therapy	0.98	0.96	0.94
Client IQ	0.69	0.69	0.60
Client age[a]	0.99	0.99	0.91
Therapist experience x neurotic diagnosis	0.76	0.75	0.70
Therapist experience x delinquent diagnosis	1.00	1.00	1.00
Internal validity	0.76	0.71	0.42
Follow-up time[b]	0.99	0.99	0.95
Outcome type[c]	0.87	0.70	0.76
Reactivity[d]	0.57	0.56	0.57
Effect size	1.00	1.00	0.78

[a]Transformed age = $(age-25) (| age-25|)^{.5}$.
[b]Transformed follow-up time = follow-up time$^{.5}$.
[c]"Other" category removed for purpose of dichotomization.
[d]Transformed reactivity = reactivity$^{2.25}$.
Source: Orwin and Cordray, 1985.

establishing interrater agreement, Table 3.5 presents a range of values (using liberal to conservative assumptions, with column 1 being the most liberal). Some variables are quite sensitive to procedural changes. Because coded characteristics determine whether a study is included or excluded, high agreement is necessary. But it is precisely such variables as internal validity that are least reliable.

For example, both Mumford, Schlesinger, and Glass (1982) and Devine and Cook (1983) examined the effects of psychosocial interventions on postoperative length of hospital stay. Although these two meta-analyses differ in important ways, they do rely on overlapping sets of studies. Substantial agreement is evident when we contrast the coded values reported by each group of authors, but there are also some important consistencies in the way they categorized studies. For instance, of the ten studies included in both meta-analyses, both groups agreed that the assignment process in eight studies was either random or nonrandom. But Devine and Cook (1983) decided that assignment in two studies had been nonrandom, while Mumford, Schlesinger, and Glass (1982) felt that it had been random. Inconsistencies in the calculations of derived effect size also were apparent in four of the twelve results reported for overlapping estimates. Whether these errors average out is unclear.

The cumulative effect of these sources of variable error has not been investigated, but it is clear that they can increase or diminish the overall precision of meta-analytic results. However, when variable error is present in breakdown variables or in variables used in multivariate analyses, these sources of error turn into bias.

Systematic Error: Sampling Issues. For survey research, Kish (1965) identified several varieties of sampling bias that are relevant to features of meta-analysis. Technical developments in the field appear to have removed one of Kish's (1965) sampling biases, and progress is being made on the other.

Biased Estimates. Hedges (1981) has provided a correction to estimates of effect sizes aimed at eliminating bias caused by small sample sizes in primary studies. The small-sample bias is important for samples of fifty or fewer, but it becomes trivial as sample sizes increase. None of the meta-analyses reviewed here made use of this correction.

Frame Bias. Frame bias is the result of inappropriate selection procedures (for example, duplication). For meta-analysis, this problem arises when studies are used to establish the population frame but multiple effect sizes are extracted from each study. Since effect sizes within studies are unlikely to be independent, either because they represent multiple measures of the same phenomena or because errors are correlated (because all assessments were carried out under the same conditions), tests of statistical significance will be incorrect. Strube (1985) shows that multiple results can substantially inflate combined Z's.

This problem was recognized by Devine and Cook (1983) and by Kavale and Forness (1983), who addressed it by reporting two sets of analyses, one based on all effect sizes, the other on an average effect size computed for each study. Several researchers have questioned the second practice on the grounds that some measures are more central to the research questions than others (Cordray and Bootzin, 1983; Paul, 1987). In any case, an average effect size within studies often has little conceptual value. Strube (1985) and Rosenthal and Rubin (1986) developed approximations for integrating multiple results from a given study. These procedures reduce overweighting of studies with multiple effects (a form of duplication in the sampling sense) and produce a more precise estimate of sampling error per study.

Systematic Error: Other Issues. Kish (1965) identified four other kinds of systematic error that are relevant to meta-analytic practices. Two—noncoverage and nonresponse—refer to nonobservations, and two—consistent processing errors and measurement problems—refer to biased observations. Here, the analogy between meta-analysis and survey research breaks down somewhat, but some parallels can be drawn. That is, whereas survey research attempts to solicit information from individuals, meta-analysis gathers its evidence from studies. Because of reporting deficiencies, these studies are not always cooperative and trustworthy. For this reason, meta-analysts encounter many of the same issues—for example, hidden populations, missing data—that survey researchers do, and the same types of practices—for example, imputation, sensitivity analysis—are needed to estimate the influence of the resulting deviations from the ideal case.

Noncoverage. Individuals or subgroups—for example, the homeless—are sometimes excluded from the sampling frame. Similarly, studies or clusters of studies can be excluded from a meta-analysis. Although there is very little evidence on whether different analysts collect the same studies, isolated cases show that it is very possible for "populations" of studies to differ between analysts (Cordray and Fischer, in press). As noted earlier, Mumford, Schlesinger, and Glass (1982) found ten studies on the effects of psychological interventions on length of hospital stay, while Devine and Cook (1983) recovered thirty-four studies by expanding the number of bibliographic data bases that they used in their search. In general, Rosenthal (1984) reports a high degree of reliability among information sources, but Dickersin and others (1985) report that fewer than two-thirds of the relevant trials appeared in a perinatal data base. The problem of failing to identify all relevant studies is referred to in the literature on meta-analysis as the *file-drawer problem* (Orwin, 1983; Rosenthal, 1979). It can result from publication bias and the failure of the primary analyst to publicize his or her findings. By making assumptions about the characteristics of studies that are excluded, we can construct several types of estimates to assess the influence of noncoverage. For example, we can calculate a fail-safe *n* indicating the number of unavailable studies that it would take to overturn the reported aggregate results. Of the seven meta-analyses discussed in the preceding section, only one—Greenhouse and others, 1990—determined the influence of the file-drawer problem. Devine and Cook (1983) estimated the influence of publication bias by comparing the results of published studies and dissertations. In both cases, the investigators found this form of bias to be inconsequential, although Greenhouse and others (1990) showed that the assumptions underlying alternative calculations had a substantial influence on the fail-safe n's that were derived.

One of the most striking features of current meta-analysis is its propensity to locate every study that was conducted, published or not, and then quickly separate the "good" studies from the "bad." The synthesis effort is then directed at the "good" studies, and the others are either excluded or not emphasized. These practices result in a form of noncoverage that the meta-analyst deliberately imposes. For some applications—for example, the study was designed to examine only the best available evidence—this decision rule is justified, but it also can limit the utility of meta-analysis for helping us to understand why interventions fail or succeed.

Meta-analysts have used a variety of definitions of quality, which in turn have determined the contents of subsets of the available studies. For example, a meta-analysis of the effects of desegregation on the achievement of black students (National Institute of Education, 1983) judged a study to be high in quality if the study design was adequate and there was evidence of well-articulated desegregation "treatment." Implicit within this definition is a conjoint inclusion rule: Only the studies (and thereby only the programs or projects) that pass both tests are included. If we look at the other side— what has been excluded—it is evident that at least three other categories of studies have been lumped together and by inference characterized as low in quality. These are depicted in Figure 3.1.

Figure 3.1. Meta-analysis and the Conjoint Inclusion Rule

		Basis for causal attribution	
		Weak	Strong
	Weak	A	B
Program implementation	Strong	C	D

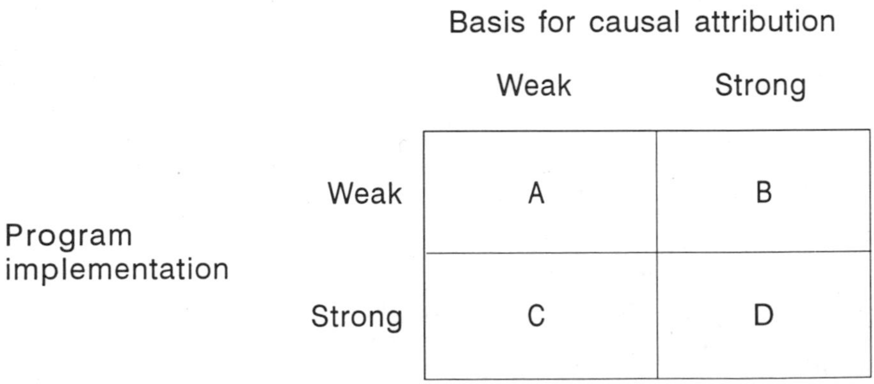

Several points can be raised about the implications of these inclusion rules. First, labeling the studies in cell D as high in methodological quality, as the National Institute of Education (1983) meta-analysis did, is misleading. Rather, the decision rule just described created a cluster of studies that we might more accurately characterize as showing strong evidence of desegregation. Consequently, the studies represented by cell D are not simply methodologically strong, they are also based on programs that are well implemented.

However, meta-analysis does not often use conjoint inclusion rules. Normally, inclusion rules that focus on the strength of the designs (cells B and D) will combine programs that vary in level of implementation. Unless we perform further stratification, effect sizes will be heterogeneous (assuming that programs are truly effective).

Nevertheless, although the conjoint inclusion rule provides a strong test of the intervention, it ignores a substantial amount of potentially valuable qualitative information about the circumstances surrounding the program and the characteristics of evaluation methods. For example, contrasting evidence from cell B with evidence from cell D provides a quasi-experimental comparison that is rather unique to meta-analysis. That is, additional probing of the differences among the studies in each cell might reveal why program implementation is weak, and corrective actions could be proposed.

Of course, program attributes (for example, implementation fidelity, intervention strength) are not dichotomous in practice. We can analyze this type of variation profitably in terms of a dose-response relationship (Howard, Kopta, Krause, and Orlinsky, 1986). Not only does this type of analysis exploit more of the available information, but it can provide policymakers, program managers, and other practitioners with guidance about the added value of increasing the strength of an intervention. For example, an analysis of the literature on programs for pregnant teenagers found no evidence that more-comprehensive services were any more effective than less-comprehensive services (U.S. General Accounting Office, 1986).

Another form of information that restrictive inclusion rules can overlook is evidence of operational problems. If one of the reasons for conducting a meta-analysis is to determine whether programs should be expanded or to identify the programs that seem most promising, restricting the meta-analysis to studies in cell D would exclude evidence about the likely shortfalls or obstacles that could be encountered in other settings. Evidence from studies in cell B could yield information on problems associated with program implementation, and evidence from studies in cell C could illuminate additional factors associated with method failures.

Inclusion rules also influence generalization. Generalization of results has always been an issue in areas where we cannot use the machinery of statistical sampling to derive a concise estimate of how far we are likely to be from the true value.

The issue of generalization is complex within a meta-analysis, where it is linked to the inclusion rules that are employed. Whereas the target of generalization is the knowledge base (that is, the number of studies undertaken), a question of greater interest may be, Does a program or treatment work? To the extent to which we have not evaluated all projects or interventions, the knowledge base does not reflect the true target population. Figure 3.2 makes this point concrete.

Figure 3.2 Influence of Inclusion Rules on Generalization

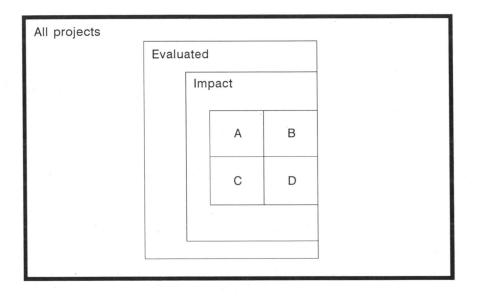

It is very unlikely that the most restrictive inclusion rule (cell D) represents the populations of interest. More important, it is impossible to speak to the issue of generalization without additional information. Crain (1984) conducted an analysis that highlights the importance of gathering and using information from other studies that is not included in the final synthesis. That is, Crain (1984) showed that, given the distribution of studies across all cells (A through D), the core of studies selected for use in the National Institute of Education (1983) meta-analysis differed in important ways that did not represent critical features of all desegregation efforts.

From a sampling perspective, these inclusion rules result in the identification of convenience samples, and generalization is very limited. Bryant and Wortman's (1984) analysis of the differences between included and excluded studies gives us a sense of the portion of the total population represented by the final selection of studies. These are the kinds of practices that will make meta-analysis more useful.

Nonresponse. A less extreme form of nonobservation is nonresponse, when the study fails to disclose important information on all or some variables of interest. At least two factors influence this type of nonobservation. The information is missing, or it has been poorly reported.

For example, for seven of thirteen studies, Greenhouse and others (1990) had to compute means and standard deviations from indirect information (or intermediate statistics) presented in the studies. In another case, they estimated these values from figures, and in three instances (not included in the meta-analysis), adequate data were not available. The authors estimated (and imputed) pre and post correlations for a partially overlapping set of seven studies. In total, ten of thirteen effect sizes that they computed relied on imputed or estimated statistics. In an effort to assess the influence of these estimates on the overall effect size, these analysts systematically used sensitivity analysis to assess the influence of each effect size value. Judging from Sacks and others (1987), this practice is rare; fewer than one in five meta-analyses reports the use of such types of assessments.

Insufficient reporting is common enough that Glass, McGaw, and Smith (1981) devote considerable space to ways of recovering effect sizes from test statistics and tables. But some studies and areas are so poorly documented that no amount of statistical conversion can recover lost information. For example, Venulet, Blattner, von Bulow, and Berneker (1982) found that only 19 percent of the studies that they considered contained all the information they needed to assess adverse drug reactions. Mosteller, Gilbert, and McPeek (1980) viewed the reporting deficiencies in clinical trials as so severe that they encouraged editors to adopt and enforce reporting standards. DerSimonian, Charette, McPeek, and Mosteller (1982) also discussed issues in reporting on methods in clinical trials.

Methodological options for dealing with these problems include using estimates from other sources, imputation, and establishment of coding conventions. Each option has its strengths and weaknesses. In general, these practices probably introduce a systematic source of bias in the statistical results. For example, substituting the mean as a way of accommodating item nonresponse systematically affects estimates of variability. One way of accounting for differential reporting is to record the level of uncertainty associated with particular information (Orwin and Cordray, 1985) and to use this information in the statistical analysis of study characteristics.

Field Errors. Since meta-analysis relies on the data reported in primary studies, aggregated results can be only as good as the studies themselves. Field errors at the level of primary studies include measurement problems (for example, reactivity) and other operational problems (for example, inaccurate enumeration or classification). Further, several authors, including Gore, Jones, and Rytter (1977), have noted that the use of statistical procedures in published studies is often questionable. For example, fifteen of the seventy-seven papers that these authors reviewed performed no statistical analysis. Of the sixty-two remaining papers, fifty-two included at least one error. Errors ranged from inadequate description of basic data to incorrect computation of basic statistical tests. None of the seven studies examined in the preceding section reported these kinds of irregularities. As is obvious, meta-analyses can suffer from the same problems (see the meta-analysis on the effects of weight loss on hypertension).

Processing Errors. Processing errors at the level of primary studies can yield systematic distortions in the basic data used for meta-analysis. The literature on synthesis has devoted considerable attention to the question of differences in results due to study characteristics. Nevertheless, processing errors are also possible. These range from consistent transcription errors (for example, coding conventions) to more controversial issues, such as the choice of standard deviations for calculating an effect size. Here, the issue is not that a choice is right or wrong but merely that a choice can influence one's results systematically. Here, too, the use of sensitivity analyses that test the robustness of results and the reporting of results derived from multiple analytical procedures may be the only justifiable tactics when statistical theory, logic, and common sense provide no guidance on how to handle these types of problems. The studies conducted by Greenhouse and others (1990) and by Devine and Cook (1983) offer good illustrations of these practices.

The cumulative influence of these potential sources of systematic error has not been assessed. However, it is clear that each of these potential biases could influence the results or undermine the credibility of a synthesis.

Summary. What is impressive about the literature on meta-analysis is that it has acknowledged so many of the issues just reviewed. Partial solutions have been developed for many of these problems, or at least we have diagnostic tests for their influence. The problems come in a variety of forms, and sound meta-analytic practices appear to be associated with direct assessments of the influence of methodological choices on the results of primary studies. Individual analysts have tested isolated aspects of these practices. Perhaps a broader conceptual framework, such as total synthesis error, will force us to attend to the variety of statistical and nonstatistical issues that the meta-analyst must face.

A Prospective Look at Meta-analysis

At the beginning of this chapter, I stated that meta-analysis can strengthen the causal interpretation of nonexperimental data. While the promise is clearly there, changes in practices at the primary and meta-analytic levels of research must occur before meta-analysis becomes as useful as it can be. Other uses of meta-analysis also seem promising provided that practices at both levels can be enhanced.

Improved Reporting. Deficiencies in reporting at the level of primary studies are pervasive, and this problem must be recognized in the meta-analytic process. More important, meta-analysis can lead to improvements in reporting, since systematic reviews of studies can highlight persistent problems. This has been well demonstrated by Mosteller, Gilbert, and McPeek (1980). Efforts like their give the field its greatest hope for improving both primary and meta-analytic research. However, for such improvement to occur, meta-analysts have to disclose the problems they encounter. With the exception of Greenhouse and others (1990), none of the meta-analyses reviewed in this chapter highlighted reporting deficiencies. It can only be speculated that the literature that the other authors reviewed was trouble free, that the analysts were clever in overcoming problems, or that problems were ignored. Without documentation, successful replication is unlikely (Bullock and Svyantek, 1985; Abrami, Cohen, and d'Apollonia, 1988; Wanous, Sullivan, and Malinak, 1989). Worse, those who know the strengths and weaknesses of the literature will not view the meta-analyses as credible (Eysenck, 1978).

Nonstatistical Meta-analytic Practices. The section of this chapter that reviewed individual meta-analyses noted several omissions. Consistent with the evidence reported by Sacks and others (1987), about half of the studies provided enough information to judge the adequacy of the literature search. In one case, expanding the number of data bases that were examined increased the number of studies to be considered by more than 200 percent. Since the number of studies considered can change the results of meta-analysis dramatically, this is a critical phase of the process that must be taken seriously. As yet, there is not much evidence on the completeness of the bibliographic data bases that we have to work with. More empirical work of the sort described by Dickersin's group (Dickersin and others, 1985; Dickersin, Min, and Meinert, 1992) seems necessary. Once studies and effect sizes have been identified, it also seems necessary to document decision rules for inclusion and exclusion of studies (Matt, 1989). Bryant and Wortman (1984) serve as a useful model of the kinds of analyses that can be conducted. It would be easy to expand this recommendation to information on the types of clients, treatment, and conditions represented by included and excluded studies. Such information would give us a more useful basis for generalization.

Quality of Coding Practices. As already noted, interrater agreement on information extracted from the study reports is rarely assessed (or at least it is rarely reported). At each phase of the meta-analytic process, judgments must be made about the inclusion of studies, the adequacy of their methods, and the credibility of results. For many meta-analytic variables, these are complex judgments, and it is unreasonable to think that individuals will not make errors. Given the heavy reliance on the judgment of analysts in meta-analysis, reliability assessments should be viewed as mandatory.

Sensitivity Analysis. Efforts to transform a body of knowledge into a meta-analytic data base require an endless number of choices and decisions. The statistical procedures that result from these choices rest, of course, on several layers of assumptions. Whether the assumptions are tenable in a particular application is often unknown or unknowable. In such cases, the robustness of the results of changes in analytical models should be assessed. The tactics used for assessing robustness are collectively referred to as *sensitivity analysis*.

Research Characteristics: General and Specific? Looking across various meta-analyses at the variables used to characterize the quality of the research, we see that few used more than a handful of indicators. These indicators can include ratings of internal validity, categorization of the reactivity of measures, specification of sample sizes and postassignment attrition levels, degree of experimental blinding, method of participant assignment, and type of comparison. To date, little attention has been devoted to the technical factors that should be included in assessments of past research and evaluations. The rating schemes developed by Chalmers and others (1981), the U.S. General Accounting Office (1978, 1990), and Mosteller, Gilbert, and McPeek (1980) are some notable exceptions. For the most part, these checklists are general in nature and simply require summary judgments.

When summary judgments are divided into their constituent parts, information about research quality becomes more useful. For example, the statistical power of a comparison can be summarized as a single value. However, evidence on the component parts—that is, the raw difference between groups, within-group variability, measurement sensitivity, sample size, and measurement error—would be more diagnostic. If sample sizes have to be restricted when a particular study is planned, a sensible alternative is to concentrate on other components that influence the sensitivity of the design (for example, matching prior to assignment, devising more sensitive measures, enhancing the strength of the intervention). Exercising these options intelligently depends on a detailed understanding of past successes and failures (Cordray and Sonnefeld, 1985).

The Potential Need for Secondary Analysis. Some of the problems noted in primary studies that lead to systematic errors in study results occur at a level that is difficult to detect simply by reviewing an author's report. Secondary analysis offers a possible means of directly assessing the accuracy and credibility of primary studies (Boruch, Wortman, and Cordray, 1981). Rather than relying on what has been reported, secondary analysis obtains and reanalyzes the data used in the primary analysis. This is a drastic solution, and it may be the most feasible if it is performed as a validation exercise that reanalyzes a sampling of studies and contrasts the results with those reported in the primary studies. The main value of such a practice is to gain a sense of the degree to which the types of errors caused by deficient reporting and technical problems influenced the synthesis process. Unfortunately, it is difficult to obtain primary results from research and evaluation that were not conducted with federal support. Nevertheless, for those studies that are available, secondary analysis is an important tool for understanding the strengths and limits of meta-analysis.

Need for Contextual Evidence. The meta-analyses examined in this chapter illustrate the difficulties and ambiguities associated with trying to determine why some studies yield large positive effects and others show negative effects. Post hoc probing for factors that account convincingly for the observed variability reveals the limits of meta-analysis. Reporting problems and noncomparability among studies resulting from confoundings associated with differences in time, treatments, measures, populations, and so forth make it very difficult (but not impossible) to answer questions about why estimates differ.

As with any observational data, one of the few ways in which we can reduce uncertainty is by measuring and modeling the factors that are believed to contribute to the observed variability. Although more advanced statistical procedures are now available, little effort has been made to develop such models. Finsterbusch's (1984) analysis of factors related to the impact of fifty-two Agency for International Development projects is one noteworthy exception. For more complex social programs, it is possible to gain a better understanding of results by examining features of the program environment. Often, the analyst must look at literature besides the studies selected for the synthesis; in certain cases, a review of legislative history can help. Yeaton and Wortman (1984) provide a useful summary of the kinds of factors that a model of change in the medical context could include.

Quantitative and Qualitative Evidence. Both quantitative and qualitative descriptions are essential if meta-analyses are to be useful. Reducing a complex design, treatment, or set of participant characteristics to numerical values probably obscures as much as it illuminates. Narrative descriptions are a necessary component of the synthesis process. For example, by looking at the descriptions of clients in the studies summarized by Prioleau, Murdock, and Brody (1983), Cordray and Bootzin (1983) concluded that the studies represented a highly select clientele (school-age children) and that the results might not be applicable to other populations of interest. Rather than belabor this point, the authors referred the reader to thoughtful discussions of the role of numbers and narrative appearing in Cook and Leviton (1980) and in Light and Pillemer (1984).

Capitalizing on the Substantial Efforts of Reviewers. As stated earlier, the most time-consuming aspect of the synthesis processes involves the reading and recording of information. This effort can be viewed as more rewarding by recognizing that many of the resulting details can be put to good use when subsequent evaluations are being planned (Cordray and Sonnefeld, 1985). Acting on this recognition requires authors and editors to see the value of devoting journal space to more complex descriptions of studies, and quantitatively oriented reviewers will have to make the details of their coding readily available to the research and evaluation community.

Development of a normative base that can be used to make planning decisions may facilitate these efforts. Some may claim that I am oversimplifying the planning process—that programs are too unpredictable to warrant extensive investments in detailed planning. However, the field may not have sufficiently considered the uncertainty that results when an analyst plunges in without first taking stock of the rich history of successful and unsuccessful practices.

Conclusions

The nature of recent comments in the literature on meta-analysis suggests a shift from skepticism to cautious acceptance. While the viability of the method was being debated, a substantial research and development effort was under way. Work by statisticians has greatly improved our understanding of the statistical properties of the method (Hedges and Olkin, 1985; Hunter and Schmidt, 1990; Rosenthal and Rubin, 1986; Strube, 1985).

As meta-analytic practices have matured, recognition of their epistemological footing has grown. That is, given that meta-analysis is an observational (in Cochran's sense) strategy, it is basically descriptive. But, as Cook and others (1992) have argued and demonstrated with their case studies, meta-analysis enables us to assess explanatory models and make increasingly broad empirically based generalizations. Learning about the robustness of primary studies and their resistance to plausible rival explanations provides a useful step toward better explanation. The suspected problems of individual studies can often be accommodated more efficiently through meta-analysis than by primary data collection, logic, or simply overlooking them.

Expanding the Knowledge Base. As a form of inquiry, meta-analysis is useful to the extent to which new studies are continually being conducted. For policy-making and applied areas, this is critical. Changes in programs and technologies, the political climate in which they operate, and the composition of the populations served mean that past research and evaluations often have limited value when we want to summarize current conditions. However, as recent events in numerous federal agencies have shown, investments in research, evaluation, and statistics have declined considerably. Thus, with resources limited, efforts have to be made to ensure that funds are well spent on high-quality primary studies. Meta-analytic procedures can assist in this regard.

Improving Practices. As quantitative syntheses become more visible in the policy-making context, the value of investing in research should become more obvious. As already noted, the inclusion rules now used often overlook a substantial amount of potentially useful information that could be used in the planning of future studies and thereby improve the quality of primary research and evaluation. Several methods could give us a better understanding of the conditions under which high-quality studies are produced. Returning to Figure 3.1, it is possible to ascertain for cells A, B, and C whether the null results can be attributed to failures in program implementation (B), failures in method (C), or failures both in program implementation and in method (A). A synthesis of information from studies in these cells could reveal the types of alterations needed to ensure that the next generation of programs and studies did not fall prey to the same errors. Cordray and Sonnefeld (1985) outline several approaches capitalizing on past research in the planning of new studies.

The review in this chapter of the sources of systematic and variable errors that can affect the synthesis process shows some of the methodological vulnerabilities of meta-analysis. A variety of procedures can be used to test the influence of decision rules, and they seem to offer the most hope for solving these types of problems, at least until the reporting of primary studies improves.

Over the past ten years, meta-analytic practice has increased dramatically in sophistication. Solutions have been developed for many of the problems identified here in the section on assessing practices. Nevertheless, not all the conceptual challenges have been met. For example, in what is considered the state of the art in evaluation research, simple pre- versus post-test assessments are being replaced with structural models that emphasize mediational mechanisms, implementation issues, estimates of the influence of exogenous factors, and so on (Cordray, 1986). Despite the increasing prominence that these models are expected to assume in the near future, little attention has been paid thus far to the problems involved in integrating the results of complex analyses. If meta-analysis is to continue to be useful in the future, it will have to keep pace with other methodological advances.

References

Abrami, P. C., Cohen, P. A., and d'Apollonia, S. "Implementation Problems in Meta-analysis." *Review of Educational Research,* 1988, *58* (2), 151–179.

Bangert-Drowns, R. L. "Review of Developments in Meta-analytic Method." *Psychological Bulletin,* 1986, *99,* 388–399.

Becker, B. J. "Models of Science Achievement: Forces Affecting Male and Female Performance in School Science." In T. D. Cook, H. Cooper, D. S. Cordray, H. Hartmann, L. V.

Hedges, R. J. Light, T. A. Louis, and F. Mosteller (eds.), *Meta-analysis for Explanation: A Casebook.* New York: Russell Sage Foundation, 1992.

Bentler, P. M. *EQS: A Structural Equations Program Manual.* Los Angeles: BMDP Statistical Software, 1989.

Boruch, R. F. "What Have We Learned About Experimental Evaluation?" In D. S. Cordray, H. S. Bloom, and R. J. Light (eds.), *Practical Lessons for Evaluation Planning and Design.* New Directions for Program Evaluation, no. 34. San Francisco: Jossey-Bass, 1987.

Boruch, R. F., Wortman, P. M., and Cordray, D. S. (eds.). *Reanalyzing Program Evaluations: Policies and Practices for Secondary Analysis of Educational and Social Programs.* San Francisco: Jossey-Bass, 1981.

Bryant, F. B., and Wortman, P. M. "Methodological Issues in the Meta-analysis of Quasi-experiments." In W. H. Yeaton and P. M. Wortman (eds.), *Issues in Data Synthesis.* New Directions for Program Evaluation, no. 24. San Francisco: Jossey-Bass, 1984.

Bullock, R. J., and Svyantek, D. J. "Analyzing Meta-analysis: Potential Problems, an Unsuccessful Replication, and Evaluation Criteria." *Journal of Applied Psychology,* 1985, *70* (1), 108–115.

Chalmers, T. C., Smith, H., Jr., Blackburn, B., Silverman, B., Schroeder, B., Reitman, D., and Ambroz, A. "A Methodology for Assessing the Quality of Randomized Control Trials." *Controlled Clinical Trials,* 1981, *2,* 31–49.

Chen, H. T. *Theory-Driven Evaluations.* Newbury Park, Calif.: Sage, 1990.

Chen, H., and Rossi, P. H. "Evaluating with Sense: A Theory-Driven Approach." *Evaluation Review,* 1983, *7,* 283–302.

Cochran, W. G. "Problems Arising in the Analysis of a Series of Similar Experiments." *Journal of the Royal Statistical Society* (supplement), 1937, *4,* 102–118.

Collins, R., and Langman, M. "Treatment with Histamine H2 Antagonists in Acute Upper Gastrointestinal Hemorrhage." *New England Journal of Medicine,* 1985, *313* (11), 660–666.

Cook, T. D., Cooper, H., Cordray, D. S., Hartmann, H., Hedges, L. V., Light, R. J., Louis, T. A., and Mosteller, F. *Meta-analysis for Explanation: A Casebook.* New York: Russell Sage Foundation, 1992.

Cook, T. D., and Leviton, L. C. "Reviewing the Literature: A Comparison of Traditional Methods with Meta-analysis." *Journal of Personality,* 1980, *48,* 449–472.

Cooper, H. M. *The Integrative Research Review: A Systematic Approach.* Newbury Park, Calif.: Sage, 1989.

Cooper, H. M., and Hedges, L. V. (eds.). *The Handbook of Research Synthesis.* New York: Russell Sage Foundation, 1994.

Cordray, D. S. "Quasi-experimental Analysis: A Mixture of Methods and Judgment." In W.M.K. Trochim (ed.), *Advances in Quasi-experimental Design and Analysis.* New Directions for Program Evaluation, no. 31. San Francisco: Jossey-Bass, 1986.

Cordray, D. S., and Bootzin, R. R. "Placebo Control Conditions: Tests of Theory or Effectiveness." *Brain and Behavioral Sciences,* 1983, *2,* 286–287.

Cordray, D. S., and Fischer, R. L. "Practical Aspects of Evaluation Synthesis and Its Variations." In J. S. Wholey, H. P. Hatry, and K. E. Newcomer (eds.), *Handbook of Practical Program Evaluation.* San Francisco: Jossey-Bass, in press.

Cordray, D. S., and Orwin, R. G. "Improving the Quality of Evidence: Interconnections Among Primary Evaluations, Secondary Analysis, and Quantitative Syntheses." In R. J. Light (ed.), *Evaluation Studies Review Annual.* Vol. 8. Newbury Park, Calif.: Sage, 1983.

Cordray, D. S., and Sonnefeld, C. J. "Quantitative Synthesis: An Actuarial Base for Planning Impact Evaluations." In D. S. Cordray (ed.), *Utilizing Prior Research in Evaluation Planning.* New Directions for Program Evaluation, no. 27. San Francisco: Jossey-Bass, 1985.

Crain, R. L. *Is Nineteen Really Better Than Ninety-Three?* Washington, D.C.: National Institute of Education, 1984.

DerSimonian, R., Charette, L. J., McPeek, B., and Mosteller, F. "Reporting on Methods in Clinical Trials." *New England Journal of Medicine,* 1982, *306,* 1332–1337.

Devine, E. C. "Effects of Psychoeducational Care with Adult Surgical Patients: A Theory-Probing Meta-analysis of Intervention Studies." In T. D. Cook, H. Cooper, D. S. Cordray, H. Hartmann, L. V. Hedges, R. J. Light, T. A. Louis, and F. Mosteller (eds.), *Meta-analysis for Explanation: A Casebook.* New York: Russell Sage Foundation, 1992.

Devine, E. C., and Cook, T. D. "Effects of Psychoeducational Interventions on Length of Postsurgical Hospital Stay: A Meta-analytic Review of Thirty-four Studies." In R. J. Light (ed.), *Evaluation Studies Review Annual.* Vol. 8. Newbury Park, Calif.: Sage, 1983.

Dickersin, K., Hewitt, P., Mutch, L., and others. "Perusing the Literature: Comparison of MEDLINE Searching with a Perinatal Clinical Trials Data Base." *Controlled Clinical Trials,* 1985, *6,* 306–307.

Dickersin, K., Min, Y., and Meinert, C. L. "Factors Influencing Publication of Research Results." *Journal of the American Medical Association,* 1992, *267* (3), 374–378.

Durlak, J. A., and Lipsey, M. W. "A Practitioner's Guide to Meta-analysis." *American Journal of Community Psychology,* 1991, *19* (3), 291–332.

Evaluation Research Society. "ERS Program Evaluation Standards." In P. H. Rossi (ed.), *Standards for Evaluation Practice.* New Directions for Program Evaluation, no. 15. San Francisco: Jossey-Bass, 1982.

Eysenck, H. J. "An Exercise in Mega-silliness." *American Psychologist,* 1978, *33,* 517.

Feingold, B. F. "Hyperkinesis and Learning Disabilities Linked to Artificial Food Flavors and Colors." *American Journal of Nursing,* 1975, *75,* 797–803.

Finsterbusch, K. *Statistical Summary of Fifty-two AID Projects: Lessons on Project Effectiveness.* College Park: University of Maryland, 1984.

Glass, G. V. "Primary, Secondary, and Meta-analysis of Research." *Educational Researcher,* 1976, *5,* 3–8.

Glass, G. V., McGaw, B., and Smith, M. L. *Meta-analysis in Social Research.* Newbury Park, Calif.: Sage, 1981.

Gore, S. M., Jones, I. G., and Rytter, E. C. "Misuse of Statistical Methods: Critical Assessments of Articles in *BMJ* from January to March 1976." *British Medical Journal,* 1977, *1,* 85–87.

Greenhouse, J. B., Fromm, D., Iyengar, S., Dew, M. A., Holland, A. L., and Kass, R. E. "The Making of a Meta-analysis: A Case Study of a Quantitative Review of Aphasia Treatment Literature." In K. Wachter and M. Staf (eds.), *The Future of Meta-analysis.* New York: Russell Sage Foundation, 1990.

Hedges, L. V. "Distribution Theory for Glass's Estimator of Effect Size and Related Estimators." *Journal of Educational Statistics,* 1981, *6,* 107–128.

Hedges, L. V. "Estimation of Effect Size from a Series of Independent Experiments." *Psychological Bulletin,* 1982, *92,* 359–369.

Hedges, L. V. "Advances in Statistical Analysis." In W. H. Yeaton and P. M. Wortman (eds.), *Issues in Data Synthesis.* New Directions for Program Evaluation, no. 24. San Francisco: Jossey-Bass, 1984.

Hedges, L. V., and Olkin, I. *Statistical Methods for Meta-analysis.* New York: Academic Press, 1985.

Hovell, M. F. "The Experimental Evidence for Weight-Loss Treatment of Essential Hypertension: A Critical Review." *American Journal of Public Health,* 1982, *72* (4), 359–368.

Howard, K. I., Kopta, S. M., Krause, M. S., and Orlinsky, D. E. "The Dose-Response Relationship in Psychotherapy." *American Psychologist,* 1986, *41* (2), 159–164.

Hunter, J. E., and Schmidt, F. L. *Methods of Meta-analysis.* Newbury Park, Calif.: Sage, 1990.

Kavale, K. A., and Forness, S. R. "Hyperactivity and Diet Treatment: A Meta-analysis of the Feingold Hypothesis." *Journal of Learning Disability,* 1983, *6,* 324–330.

Kish, L. *Survey Sampling.* New York: Wiley, 1965.

Leamer, E. E. *Specification Searches: Ad Hoc Inference with Nonexperimental Data*. New York: Wiley, 1978.

Light, R. J., and Pillemer, D. B. *Summing Up: The Science of Reviewing Research*. Cambridge, Mass.: Harvard University Press, 1984.

Lipsey, M. W. *Design Sensitivity: Statistical Power for Experimental Research*. Newbury Park, Calif.: Sage, 1990.

Lipsey, M. W. "Juvenile Delinquency Treatment: A Meta-analytic Inquiry into the Variability of Effects." In T. D. Cook, H. Cooper, D. S. Cordray, H. Hartmann, L. V. Hedges, R. J. Light, T. A. Louis, and F. Mosteller (eds.), *Meta-analysis for Explanation: A Casebook*. New York: Russell Sage Foundation, 1992.

Lipsey, M. W., Crosse, S., Dunkle, J., and others. "Evaluation: The State of the Art and the Sorry State of the Science." In D. S. Cordray (ed.), *Utilizing Prior Research in Evaluation Planning*. New Directions for Program Evaluation, no. 27. San Francisco: Jossey-Bass, 1985.

Louis, T. A., Fineberg, H. V., and Mosteller, F. "Findings for Public Health from Meta-analysis." *Annual Review of Public Health*, 1985, *6*, 1–20.

Mantel, N., and Haenszel, W. "Statistical Aspects of the Analysis of Data from Retrospective Studies of Disease." *Journal of the National Cancer Institute*, 1959, *22*, 719–748.

Matt, G. E. "Decision Rules for Selecting Effect Sizes in Meta-analysis: A Review and Reanalysis of Psychotherapy Outcome Studies." *Psychological Bulletin*, 1989, *105* (1), 106–115.

Mosteller, F., Gilbert, J. P., and McPeek, B. "Reporting Standards and Research Strategies for Controlled Trials: Agenda for the Editor." *Controlled Clinical Trials*, 1980, *1*, 37–58.

Mumford, E., Schlesinger, H. J., and Glass, G. V. "The Effects of Psychological Intervention on Recovery from Surgery and Heart Attacks: An Analysis of the Literature." *American Journal of Public Health*, 1982, *72* (2), 141–151.

National Institute of Education. *The Effects of School Desegregation on the Achievement of Black Students*. Unpublished report, National Institute of Education, Washington, D.C., 1983.

Orwin, R. G. "A Fail-Safe *n* for Effect Sizes." *Journal of Educational Statistics*, 1983, *8*, 157–159.

Orwin, R. G., and Cordray, D. S. "Effects of Deficient Reporting on Meta-analysis: A Conceptual Framework and Reanalysis." *Psychological Bulletin*, 1985, *97*, 134–147.

Paul, G. L. "Can Pregnancy Be a Placebo Effect? Terminology, Design, and Conclusions in the Study of Psychological and Pharmacological Treatments of Behavioral Disorders." In L. White, B. Tursky, and G. F. Schwartz (eds.), *Placebo: Clinical Phenomena and New Insights*. New York: Guilford, 1987.

Prioleau, L., Murdock, M., and Brody, N. "An Analysis of Psychotherapy Versus Placebo Studies." *Brain and Behavioral Sciences*, 1983, *4*, 1–30.

Rindskopf, D. "New Developments in Selection Modeling for Quasi-experimentation." In W.M.K. Trochim (ed.), *Advances in Quasi-experimental Design and Analysis*. New Directions for Program Evaluation, no. 31. San Francisco: Jossey-Bass, 1986.

Rosenthal, R. "The 'File-Drawer Problem' and the Tolerance for Null Results." *Psychological Bulletin*, 1979, *86*, 638–641.

Rosenthal, R. *Meta-analytic Procedures for Social Research*. Newbury Park, Calif.: Sage, 1984.

Rosenthal, R., and Rubin, D. B. "Comparing Effect Sizes of Independent Studies." *Psychological Bulletin*, 1982, *92*, 500–504.

Rosenthal, R., and Rubin, D. B. "Meta-analytic Procedures for Combining Studies with Multiple Effect Sizes." *Psychological Bulletin*, 1986, *99* (3), 400–406.

Sackett, P. R., Schmitt, N., Tenopyr, M. L., and others. "Commentary on Forty Questions About Validity Generalization and Meta-analysis." *Personnel Psychology*, 1985, *38*, 697–798.

Sacks, H. S., Berrier, J., Reitman, D., and others. "Meta-analysis of Randomized Controlled

Trials." *New England Journal of Medicine,* 1987, *316* (8), 450–455.

Sacks, H. S., Chalmers, T. C., and Smith, H. "Randomized Versus Historical Controls for Clinical Trials." *American Journal of Medicine,* 1982, *72,* 233–240.

Schmidt, F. L., Hunter, J. E., Pearlman, K., and Hirsh, H. R. "Forty Questions About Validity Generalization and Meta-analysis." *Personnel Psychology,* 1985, *38,* 697–798.

Sechrest, L., and Yeaton, W. H. "Magnitudes of Experimental Effects in Social Science Research." *Evaluation Review,* 1982, *6,* 579–600.

Shadish, W. R. "Do Family and Marital Psychotherapies Change What People Do? A Meta-analysis of Behavioral Outcomes." In T. D. Cook, H. Cooper, D. S. Cordray, H. Hartmann, L. V. Hedges, R. J. Light, T. A. Louis, and F. Mosteller (eds.), *Meta-analysis for Explanation: A Casebook.* New York: Russell Sage Foundation, 1992.

Shadish, W. R., Jr., Cook, T. D., and Houts, A. C. "Quasi-experimentation in a Critical Multiplist Mode." In W.M.K. Trochim (ed.), *Advances in Quasi-experimental Design and Analysis.* New Directions for Program Evaluation, no. 31. San Francisco: Jossey-Bass, 1986.

Shakih, W., Vayda, E., and Feldman, W. "A Systematic Review of Literature on Evaluative Studies of Tonsillectomy and Adenoidectomy." *Pediatrics,* 1976, *577* (3), 401–407.

Slavin, R. E. "Best-Evidence Synthesis: An Alternative to Meta-analytic and Traditional Reviews." *Educational Researcher,* 1986, *15,* 5–11.

Smith, M. L., Glass, G. V., and Miller, T. I. *Benefits of Psychotherapy.* Baltimore, Md.: Johns Hopkins University Press, 1980.

Stigler, S. M. *The History of Statistics: The Measurement of Uncertainty Before 1900.* Cambridge, Mass.: Harvard University Press, 1986.

Strube, M. J. "Combining and Comparing Significance Levels from Nonindependent Hypothesis Tests." *Psychological Bulletin,* 1985, *97,* 334–341.

Trochim, W.M.K., and Visco, R. J. "Quality Control in Evaluation." In D. S. Cordray (ed.), *Utilizing Prior Research in Evaluation Planning.* New Directions for Program Evaluation, no. 27. San Francisco: Jossey-Bass, 1985.

U.S. General Accounting Office. *Assessing Social Program Impact Evaluations: A Checklist Approach.* Washington, D.C.: U.S. General Accounting Office, 1978.

U.S. General Accounting Office. *Evaluation Synthesis.* Methods Paper 1. Washington, D.C.: U.S. General Accounting Office, 1983.

U.S. General Accounting Office. *Teenage Pregnancy: 500,000 Births yet Few Tested Programs.* GAO/PEMD-86-16BR. Washington, D.C.: U.S. General Accounting Office, 1986.

U.S. General Accounting Office. *Prospective Evaluation Methods: The Prospective Evaluation Synthesis.* Transfer Paper 10.1.10. Washington, D.C.: U.S. General Accounting Office, 1990.

Venulet, J., Blattner, R., von Bulow, J., and Berneker, G. G. "How Good Are Articles on Adverse Drug Reactions?" *British Medical Journal,* 1982, *284,* 252–254.

Wachter, K., and Straf, M. (eds.). *The Future of Meta-analysis.* New York: Russell Sage Foundation, 1990.

Wanous, J. P., Sullivan, S. E., and Malinak, J. "The Role of Judgment Calls in Meta-analysis." *Journal of Applied Psychology,* 1989, *74* (2), 259–264.

Wolins, L. "Responsibility for Raw Data." *American Psychologist,* 1962, *17,* 657–658.

Wortman, P. M., and Yeaton, W. H. "Synthesis of Results in Controlled Trials of Coronary Artery Bypass Graft Surgery." In R. J. Light (ed.), *Evaluation Studies Review Annual.* Vol. 8. Newbury Park, Calif.: Sage, 1983.

Yeaton, W. H., and Wortman, P. M. "Evaluation Issues in Medical Research Synthesis." In W. H. Yeaton and P. M. Wortman (eds.), *Issues in Data Synthesis.* New Directions for Program Evaluation, no. 24. San Francisco: Jossey-Bass, 1984.

DAVID S. CORDRAY is professor of public policy and psychology at Vanderbilt University, Nashville, Tennessee, and director of the Center for the Study of At-Risk Populations and Public Assistance Policy at the Vanderbilt Institute for Public Policy Studies.

INDEX

Ordering Information

NEW DIRECTIONS FOR PROGRAM EVALUATION is a series of paperback books that presents the latest techniques and procedures for conducting useful evaluation studies of all types of programs. Books in the series are published quarterly in Spring, Summer, Fall, and Winter and are available for purchase by subscription and individually.

SUBSCRIPTIONS for 1993 cost $54.00 for individuals (a savings of 34 percent over single-copy prices) and $75.00 for institutions, agencies, and libraries. Please do not send institutional checks for personal subscriptions. Standing orders are accepted.

SINGLE COPIES cost $17.95 when payment accompanies order. (California, New Jersey, New York, and Washington, D.C., residents please include appropriate sales tax.) Billed orders will be charged postage and handling.

DISCOUNTS for quantity orders are available. Please write to the address below for information.

ALL ORDERS must include either the name of an individual or an official purchase order number. Please submit your order as follows:
    Subscriptions: specify series and year subscription is to begin
    Single copies: include individual title code (such as PE1)

MAIL ALL ORDERS TO:
    Jossey-Bass Publishers
    350 Sansome Street
    San Francisco, California 94104-1310

FOR SINGLE-COPY SALES OUTSIDE OF THE UNITED STATES CONTACT:
    Maxwell Macmillan International Publishing Group
    866 Third Avenue
    New York, New York 10022

FOR SUBSCRIPTION SALES OUTSIDE OF THE UNITED STATES, contact any international subscription agency or Jossey-Bass directly.